THE KEY

STUDENT STUDY GUIDE

Science 3

THE KEY student study guide is designed to help students achieve success in school. The content in each study guide is 100% curriculum aligned and serves as an excellent source of material for review and practice. To create this book, teachers, curriculum specialists, and assessment experts have worked closely to develop the instructional pieces that explain each of the key concepts for the course. The practice questions and sample tests have detailed solutions that show problem-solving methods, highlight concepts that are likely to be tested, and point out potential sources of errors. ***THE KEY*** is a complete guide to be used by students throughout the school year for reviewing and understanding course content, and to prepare for assessments.

Published 2008

Rao,Gautam,1961 –
THE KEY – Ontario Science 3 (2009 Edition)

1. Science – Juvenile Literature. I. Title

Castle Rock Research Corp.
2340 Manulife Place
10180 – 101 Street
Edmonton, AB T5J 3S4

1 2 3 FP 10 09 08

Printed in Canada

Publisher
Gautam Rao

Contributors
Pamela Brierley
Jill Hickson
Jodie Mackie
Jared MacLeod
Mary-Ann Perras
Jennifer Walsh

Dedicated to the memory of Dr. V. S. Rao

THE KEY—Grade 3 Science

THE KEY consists of the following sections:

KEY Tips for Being Successful at School gives examples of study and review strategies. It includes information about learning styles, study schedules, and note taking for test preparation.

Class Focus includes a unit on each area of the curriculum. Units are divided into sections, each focusing on one of the specific expectations, or main ideas, that students must learn about in that unit. Examples, definitions, and visuals help to explain each main idea. Practice questions on the main ideas are also included. At the end of each unit is a test on the important ideas covered. The practice questions and unit tests help students identify areas they know and those they need to study more. They can also be used as preparation for tests and quizzes. Most questions are of average difficulty, though some are easy and some are hard—the harder questions are called *Challenger Questions*. Each unit is prefaced by a ***Table of Correlations,*** which correlates questions in the unit (and in the practice tests at the end of the book) to the specific curriculum expectations. Answers and solutions are found at the end of each unit.

KEY Strategies for Success on Tests helps students get ready for tests. It shows students different types of questions they might see, word clues to look for when reading them, and hints for answering them.

Practice Tests includes one to three tests based on the entire course. They are very similar to the format and level of difficulty that students may encounter on final tests. In some regions, these tests may be reprinted versions of official tests, or reflect the same difficulty levels and formats as official versions. This gives students the chance to practice using real-world examples. Answers and complete solutions are provided at the end of the section.

For the complete curriculum document (including specific expectations along with examples and sample problems), visit http://www.edu.gov.on.ca/eng/curriculum/elementary/subjects.html.

THE KEY *Study Guides* are available for many courses. Check www.castlerockresearch.com for a complete listing of books available for your area.

For information about any of our resources or services, please call Castle Rock Research at 905.625.3332 or toll free at 1.800.840.6224 or visit our website at http://www.castlerockresearch.com.

At Castle Rock Research, we strive to produce an error-free resource. If you should find an error, please contact us so that future editions can be corrected.

CONTENTS

Success at School

KEY FACTORS CONTRIBUTING TO SCHOOL SUCCESS

In addition to learning the content of your courses, there are some other things that you can do to help you do your best at school. Some of these strategies are listed below.

- **ATTEND SCHOOL REGULARLY** so you do not miss any classes, notes, or important activities that will help you learn.
- **KEEP A POSITIVE ATTITUDE.** Always look at what you can already do and what you already know.
- **BE PREPARED TO LEARN.** Have your pencils, pens, notebooks, and other required materials with you in class.
- **COMPLETE ALL OF YOUR ASSIGNMENTS.** Do your best to finish all of your assignments. Even if you know the material, practice will reinforce your knowledge. If an assignment or question is difficult for you, work through it as far as you can so that your teacher can see exactly where you are having difficulty.
- **SET SMALL GOALS** for yourself when you are learning new material. For example, in learning the names of minerals, do not try to learn them all in one night. Work on only one set of names each study session. When you have memorized that set, move on to another one until you have memorized all the names of minerals that you have to know.
- **REVIEW YOUR CLASSROOM WORK** regularly at home to be sure you understand the material you learned in class.
- **ASK YOUR TEACHER FOR HELP** when you do not understand something or when you are having difficulty completing your assignments.
- **GET PLENTY OF REST AND EXERCISE.** Concentrating in class is hard work. It is important to be well-rested and have time to relax and socialize with your friends. This helps you to keep a positive attitude about your school work.
- **EAT HEALTHY MEALS.** A balanced diet keeps you healthy and gives you the energy you need for studying at school and at home.

HOW TO FIND YOUR LEARNING STYLE

Every student has a certain manner in which it seems easier for him or her to learn. The manner in which you learn best is called your learning style. By knowing your learning style, you can increase your success at school. Most students use a combination of learning styles.

Do you know what type of learner you are? Read the following descriptions. Which of these common learning styles do you use most often?

- **Do you need to say things aloud?** You may learn best by saying, hearing, and seeing words. You are probably really good at memorizing dates, places, names, and facts. To learn the steps in a process, a formula, or the actions that lead up to a significant event, you may need **to write them and then read them aloud**.

- **Do you need to read or see things?** You may learn best by looking at and working with pictures. You are probably really good at puzzles, imagining things, and reading maps and charts. You may need to use strategies like **mind mapping and webbing** to organize your information and study notes.

- **Do you need to draw or write things down?** You may learn best by touching, moving, and figuring things out using manipulatives. You are probably really good at physical activities and learning through movement. You may need to ***trace*** **your finger over a diagram** to remember it, ***tap out*** **the steps** needed to solve a problem, or ***feel*** **yourself writing** or typing a formula.

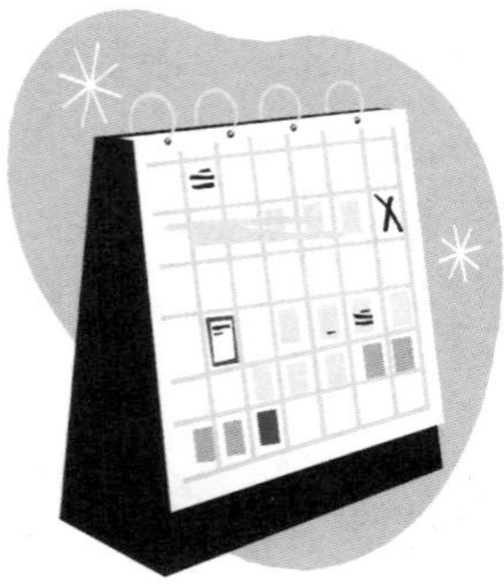

SCHEDULING STUDY TIME

You should review your class notes regularly to be sure you have a clear understanding of all the new material you have learned. Reviewing your lessons on a regular basis helps you to learn and remember ideas and concepts. It also reduces the amount of material you need to study prior to a test. Creating a study schedule will help you to make the best use of your time.

Regardless of the type of study schedule you use, you may want to consider the following strategies for making the most of your study time and effort:

- Organize your work so you begin with the most challenging material first.
- Divide the subject content into small, manageable chunks.
- Alternate regularly between different subjects and types of study activities in order to maintain your interest and motivation.
- Make a daily list with the headings *must do*, *should do*, and *could do*.
- Begin each study session by quickly reviewing what you studied the day before.
- Maintain your usual routine of eating, sleeping, and exercising to help you concentrate better for extended periods of time.

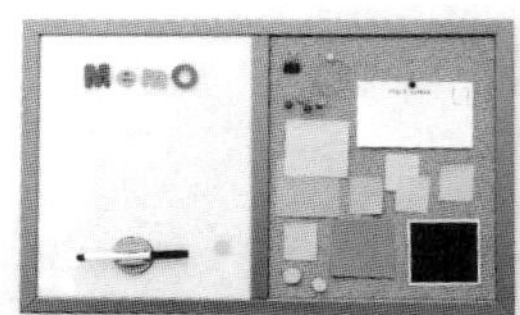

Creating Study Notes

Mind-Mapping or Webbing

- Use the key words, ideas, or concepts from your class notes to create a *mind map* or *web*, which is a diagram or visual representation of the given information. A mind map or web is sometimes referred to as a *knowledge map*.
- Write the key word, concept, theory, or formula in the centre of your page.
- Write down related facts, ideas, events, and information, and then link them to the central concept.
- Use coloured markers, underlining, or other symbols to emphasize things such as relationships, timelines, and information of importance.

Here is an example of a mind map you can use to help you learn a term.

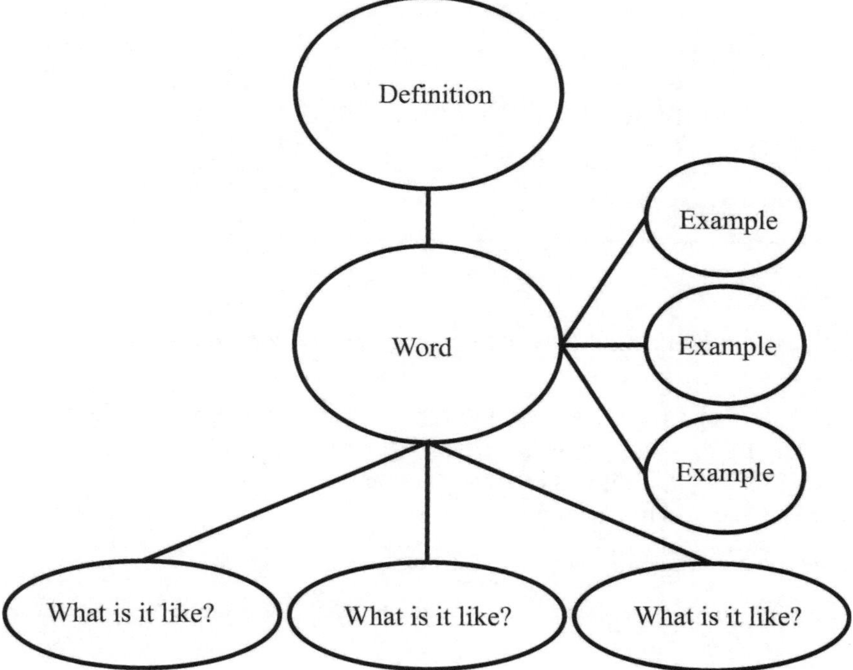

Index Cards

To use index cards while studying, follow these steps:

- Write a key word or question on the front of an index card.
- On the back of the card, write the definition of the word, the answer to the question, or any other important information you want to remember.

What is an organism?

What is an organism?

An organism is a living thing.

For example, a plant or an animal.

Symbols and Sticky Notes—Identifying Important Information

- Use symbols to mark your class notes. For example, an exclamation mark (!) might be used to point out something that must be learned well because it is a very important idea. A question mark (?) may highlight something you are not certain about, and a diamond (◊) or asterisk (*) could mark interesting information you want to remember.
- Use sticky notes when you are not allowed to mark books.
- Use sticky notes to mark a page in a book that contains an important diagram, formula, explanation, etc.
- Use sticky notes to mark important facts in research books.

Memorization Techniques

- **Association** relates new learning to something you already know. For example, stalactite and a stalagmite are the cone-shaped mineral deposits found hanging from the roof or growing up from the floor of a cave. To remember the difference between them, notice that the stalactite has a *c* in its spelling. Use the *c* to remember that stalactites come from the ceiling. Use the *g* to remember that stalagmites come from the ground.

- **Mnemonic Devices** are memory tools you create to remember a list or group of items. For example, the letters in the name *ROY G. BIV* can help you to remember the correct order and names of the colours in a rainbow or spectrum: Red, Orange, Yellow, Green, Blue, Indigo, and Violet.

- **Acronyms** are words that are formed from the first letters or parts of the words in a group. For example, *RADAR* is an acronym for Radio Detecting And Ranging; *SONAR* is an acronym for Sound Navigation And Ranging; and *NIMBY* is an acronym for not in my backyard.

- **Visualizing** requires you to use your mind's eye to *see* a chart, list, map, diagram, or sentence as it is in your textbook or notes, on the board or computer screen, or in a display.

- **Initialisms** are abbreviations that are formed from the first letters or parts of the words in a group. Unlike acronyms, initialisms cannot be pronounced as a word themselves. For example, *LED* is an initialism for Light Emitting Diode.

KEY Strategies for Reviewing

Reviewing textbook material, class notes, and handouts should be an ongoing activity. Spending time reviewing becomes more critical when you prepare for tests. You may find some of the following review strategies useful when studying during your scheduled study time.

- Before reviewing a unit, note the headings, charts, graphs, and chapter questions.
- Read the complete introduction to identify the key information that is addressed in the selection.
- Read the first sentence of the next paragraph for the main idea.
- Skim the paragraph and note key words, phrases, and information.
- Read the last sentence of the paragraph.
- Repeat the process for each paragraph and section until you have skimmed the entire selection.

KEY STRATEGIES FOR SUCCESS—A CHECKLIST

Review, review, review: that is a huge part of doing well at school and preparing for tests. Below is a checklist for you to keep track of how many suggested strategies for success you already use. Read each question and then put a check mark (✓) in the correct column. Look at the questions for which you have checked the *No* column. Think about how you might try using some of these strategies to help you do your best at school.

***KEY* Strategies for Success**	**Yes**	**No**
Do you attend school regularly?		
Do you know your personal learning style—how you learn best?		
Do you spend 15 to 30 minutes each day reviewing your notes?		
Do you study in a quiet place at home?		
Do you clearly mark the most important ideas in your study notes?		
Do you use sticky notes to mark texts and research books?		
Do you practice answering multiple-choice and written-response questions?		
Do you ask your teacher for help when you need it?		
Do you maintain a healthy diet and sleep routine?		
Do you participate in regular physical activity?		

Growth & Changes in Plants

Life Systems: Growth and Changes in Plants

Table of Correlations

	Specific Expectation	Practice Questions	Unit Test Questions
3LS1:STSE	Assess ways in which plants have an impact on society and the environment, and ways in which human activity has an impact on plant habitats;		
3LS1.1	*assess ways in which plants are important to humans and other living things, taking different points of view into consideration, and suggest ways in which humans can protect plants*	1, 2	1
3LS1.2	*assess the impact of different human activities on plants, and list personal action they can take to minimize harmful effects and enhance good effects*	3, 4	2
3LS3:Concepts	Demonstrate an understanding that plants grow and change and have distinct characteristics.		
3LS3.1	*describe the basic needs of plants, including air, water, light, warmth, and space*	5	3
3LS3.2	*identify the major parts of plants, including root, stem, flower, stamen, pistil, leaf, seed, and fruit, and describe how each contributes to the plant's survival within the plant's environment*	8	4, 5
3LS3.3	*describe the changes that different plants undergo in their life cycles*	11, 12	6, 7
3LS3.4	*describe how most plants get energy to live directly from the sun and how plants help other living things to get energy from the sun*	14, 15	8, 9
3LS3.5	*describe ways in which humans from various cultures, including Aboriginal people, use plants for food, shelter, medicine, and clothing*	16, 17	10
3LS3.6	*describe ways in which plants and animals depend on each other*	18, 19	11
3LS3.7	*describe the different ways in which plants are grown for food, and explain the advantages and disadvantages of locally grown and organically produced food, including environmental benefits*	20, 21	12
3LS3.8	*identify examples of environmental conditions that may threaten plant and animal survival*	22, 23	13
3LS2:Skills	Investigate similarities and differences in the characteristics of various plants, and ways in which the characteristics of plants relate to the environment in which they grow;		
3LS2.1	*follow established safety procedures during science and technology investigations*	24	14
3LS2.2	*observe and compare the parts of a variety of plants*	9, 10	15
3LS2.3	*germinate seeds and record similarities and differences as seedlings develop*	13	16
3LS2.4	*investigate ways in which a variety of plants adapt and/or react to their environment, including changes in their environment, using a variety of methods*	25, 26	17
3LS2.5	*use scientific inquiry/experimentation skills, and knowledge acquired from previous investigations, to investigate a variety of ways in which plants meet their basic needs*	6, 7	18, 19
3LS2.6	*use appropriate science and technology vocabulary, including stem, leaf, root, pistil, stamen, flower, adaptation, and germination, in oral and written communication*	27	20

3LS1.1 *assess ways in which plants are important to humans and other living things, taking different points of view into consideration, and suggest ways in which humans can protect plants*

The Importance of Plants to People and Other Living Things

People and animals eat plants. The plants are their food. They cannot live without plants.

Vegetarians are people who choose not to eat meat. Plants are very important to a vegetarian. They are their main source of food.

People and animals need to breathe oxygen. Plants make oxygen. People and animals breathe out carbon dioxide. Plants need carbon dioxide to make their food. They use the carbon dioxide from people and animals to make food.

Cars and other machines give off carbon dioxide. The plants in gardens and parks use the carbon dioxide in the air. This brings down the amount of carbon dioxide in the air. Too much carbon dioxide in the air can harm the environment. Trees and plants help get rid of some of this extra carbon dioxide.

A construction company builds buildings. They use wood to build a frame for a house. Plywood is used for the outer walls and floors of a house. The wood comes from trees.

People like gardens. Many gardeners find working in their garden relaxing. Some people grow fruits or vegetables in their garden. Animals like gardens too. They provide a home or a source of food for some insects and birds.

Parks and gardens in the city can lower carbon dioxide levels.

Planting tall trees around your home can lower your use of energy. Tall trees provide shade in the summer. They can protect your home from cold winds in the winter. You can buy trees from a nursery. A **nursery** is a business that grows and sells plants. Nurseries sell trees, shrubs, vegetables, and flowers.

How People Protect Plants

The most important way people can protect plants is by protecting their habitat. A **habitat** is where a plant lives—its home. Many plants are lost because people clear land to build more homes or farms. Forests around the world are being cleared to make more room for people.

Many cities are now making taller buildings. This way, they do not have to cut down trees or forests for new buildings. Many cities are also planting trees and gardens and making parks inside the city. This makes the city more beautiful, but it also helps both plants and people.

Practice

1. Travis knew that one reason plants are important to humans is that plants provide humans with

   A. glass　　B. metal　　C. plastic　　D. lumber

Use the following information to answer the next question

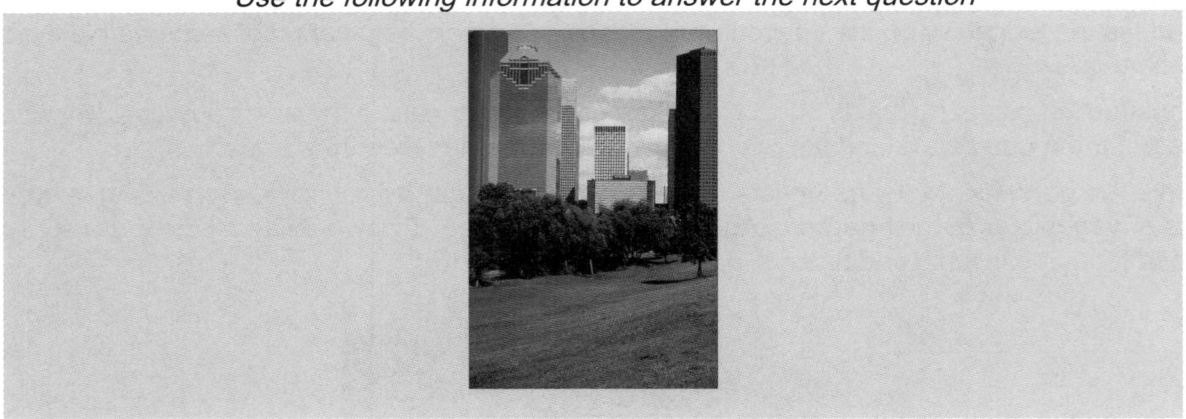

2. The plants in this area **most likely** help to

   A. stop animals from living in the city

   B. provide lumber to build houses in the city

   C. lower the carbon dioxide levels in the city

   D. make food for the people who live in the city

3LS1.2 *assess the impact of different human activities on plants, and list personal action they can take to minimize harmful effects and enhance good effects*

Helping Plants

People grow plants in pots inside their houses. They give the plants the correct soil and amount of water needed. Keeping plants in your home is good for you. Many common houseplants clean the air in your home.

If you go camping or hiking with your family, be sure to stay on trails. Walking or driving over plants may damage them. You never know when you may accidentally step on a plant that is endangered. Do not pick wildflowers. Do not dig up plants to take home. Plants do best in their natural habitat. It may seem harmless to take just one plant home. But if everyone took just one plant home, soon there would be no plants left in that area.

If you have a garden, use plants that grow naturally in your area. They have adapted to the climate and have defences against native pests. **Non-native plants** may need extra care. This extra care can use up resources needed by other plants.

Some non-native plants have escaped people's gardens and have invaded natural areas. These non-native plants can choke out **native plants**. Non-native plants may have no pests to keep their population under control. They spread and take over entire areas.

Use the following information to answer the next question

3. Plants like these are a good idea because they can
   - **A.** clean the air inside your home
   - **B.** create a habitat for animals
   - **C.** produce vegetables
   - **D.** be burned for heat

4. Teri wants to plant a garden in her yard. It is important for her only to use native plants in the garden because non-native plants
   - **A.** do not look as good
   - **B.** produce less food to eat
   - **C.** do not have the ability to grow in gardens
   - **D.** could escape and spread over an entire area

3LS3.1 *describe the basic needs of plants, including air, water, light, warmth, and space*

3LS2.5 *use scientific inquiry/experimentation skills, and knowledge acquired from previous investigations, to investigate a variety of ways in which plants meet their basic needs*

The Basic Needs of Plants

Plants, like all living things, need air, water, food, shelter, and space.

Air

Plants need air. Living things need the oxygen from the air to live. Plants use the carbon dioxide in the air to make their food. Most plants take in air through their leaves.

Water

Plants need water. Water is needed to make a plant's food. Roots bring in the water from the ground. The water has minerals in it that the plant needs to grow. There are tubes in the stems that carry the water to the leaves. When plants do not get enough water, they wilt or droop.

A plant wilts if it does not have enough water.

Food

Plants need food just like you do. But unlike you, they make their own food. To make their food, they need light, water, and carbon dioxide. Some plants need lots of light, while some need only a little. The leaves of a plant are where the food is made. In the leaves, light energy is used to change water and carbon dioxide to food.

Shelter

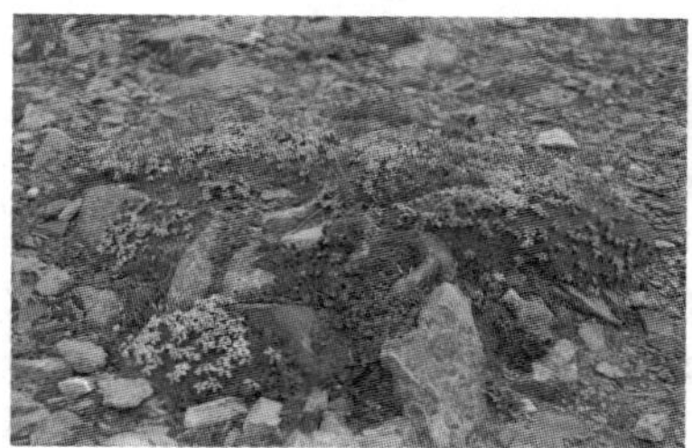

Mountain plants that grow low to the ground stay warmer

Plants that do not live in houses need protection from the wind and cold. Some plants only grow in sheltered places. They may grow between rocks. They may grow under much larger plants, such as trees. Plants that live in the Arctic or on the top of a mountain grow low to the ground. This protects them from the cold wind and crushing snow. In the summer when the sun heats the earth, these plants are closer to the heated ground.

Space

All living things need space. A plant starts out as a seed, but as it gets bigger, it needs enough room to grow. Plants compete with one another for water, light, and minerals. The space they live in has to have enough for all the plants there.

Practice

5. The roots help a plant to survive by

A. absorbing sunlight

B. taking in carbon dioxide

C. making food for the plant

D. bringing up minerals from the soil

Use the following information to answer the next question

Julie had a potted plant outside on her deck. Then she brought the plant inside and put it in a dark room. Julie continued to water it, but after a few days, the plant died.

6. The **most likely** reason that Julie's plant died when she brought it inside was
   A. there was not enough space in the pot for the plant to survive
   B. there was too much air in the house for the plant to survive
   C. the plant died because it did not get any sunlight
   D. the plant died because it did not get any fertilizer

Use the following information to answer the next question

Plants can only grow if their needs are met. One of their needs is shelter. Plants can live in cold places like the Arctic or on top of mountains.

7. Plants survive in cold places because they
   A. grow very tall to get as much sun as possible
   B. collect water with their very large leaves
   C. grow low to the ground to stay warm
   D. have waxy coverings on their leaves

3LS2.2 *observe and compare the parts of a variety of plants*

3LS3.2 *identify the major parts of plants, including root, stem, flower, stamen, pistil, leaf, seed, and fruit, and describe how each contributes to the plant's survival within the plant's environment*

The Parts of Plants

There are many different kinds of plants. No matter what they look like, most plants have the same basic parts. The major parts in most plants are the roots, stem, leaves, and flowers.

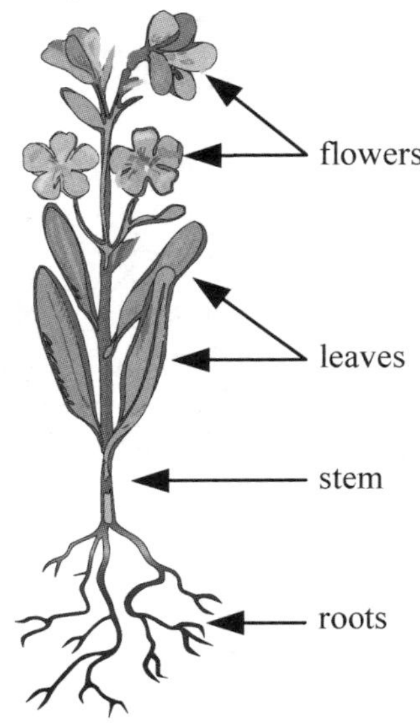

The parts of a plant

The Flower

The **flower** is where the seeds of a plant are made. The end of the **stamen** is covered in pollen. The pollen is moved from flower to flower by wind or insects. An insect might brush up against the stamen. The pollen sticks to its body. The insect flies to the next flower. The pollen brushes off the insect's body. The pollen sticks to the **pistil**, and the flower is able to make fruit. The fruit has the seeds inside. The seeds might one day make a new plant.

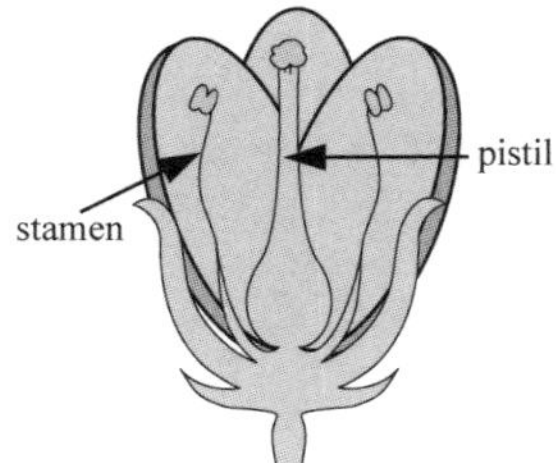

The parts of a flower

Roots

The **roots** hold the plant in the ground. They also take in water and mineral nutrients (chemicals) from the soil. Some plants have roots that store sugar. The sugar is food for the plant.

The roots of grass are small, and there are many of them. The roots are thin like hairs. They do not go very deep in the soil.

The root of a dandelion is called a tap root. The root is large and can go very deep to find water and mineral nutrients.

A carrot is a root. It stores food energy for the plant. People like to eat the root of a carrot plant. The food energy stored there is good for people too.

Stems

The **stem** holds the plant up to the light. The stem also has tubes that move water and mineral nutrients up from the roots to all the parts of the plant.

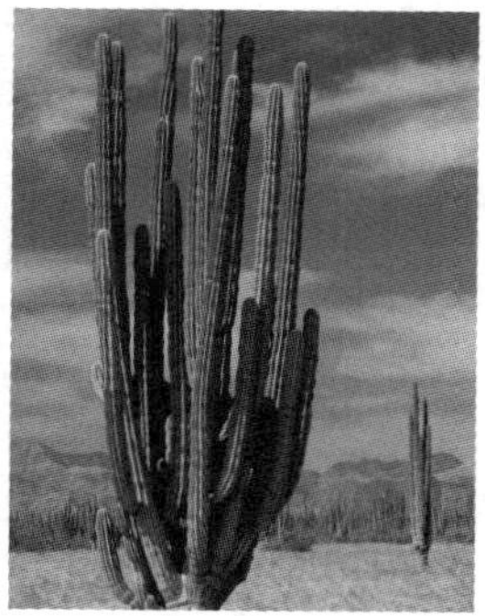

It does not rain in the desert very often. The stem of a cactus can store water for a long time.

The stem of a carnation is long and thin. It holds up the plant. Water and chemicals from the soil travel through the stem.

The stem of a tree is very hard and is covered in bark. Every year a tree lives, it adds a new layer to its stem. When a tree dies, you can count the rings and see how old it is.

LEAVES

The **leaf** of a plant takes in energy from the sun. It also takes in carbon dioxide gas from the air. Water and mineral nutrients (chemicals) from the soil travel through the stem to the leaf. The leaf uses the energy from the sun to turn them into food for the plant.

The leaves of a geranium plant are round. They are found all along the stem of the plant.

The leaves of a spider plant are long and narrow. They grow from the bottom of the plant.

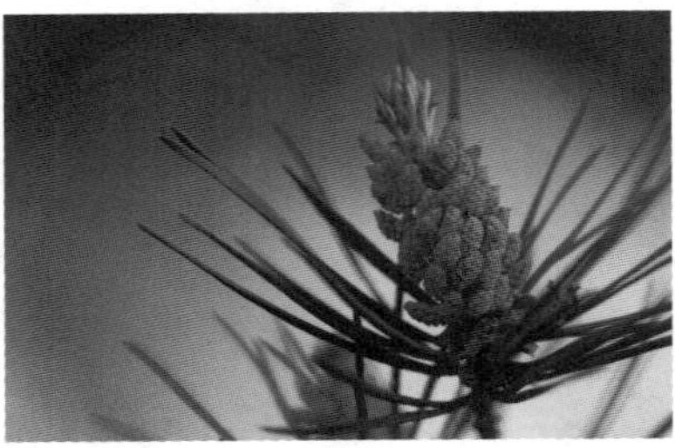

The leaves of a pine tree are called needles. They are long and very thin. They look like sewing needles. They grow all over the branches of the tree.

Practice

CHALLENGER QUESTION

Use the following information to answer the next question

8. Pollen sticks to the pistil of a flower, and the flower is able to make fruit. The pistil is shown by arrow

   A. 1 **B.** 2 **C.** 3 **D.** 4

CHALLENGER QUESTION

Use the following information to answer the next question

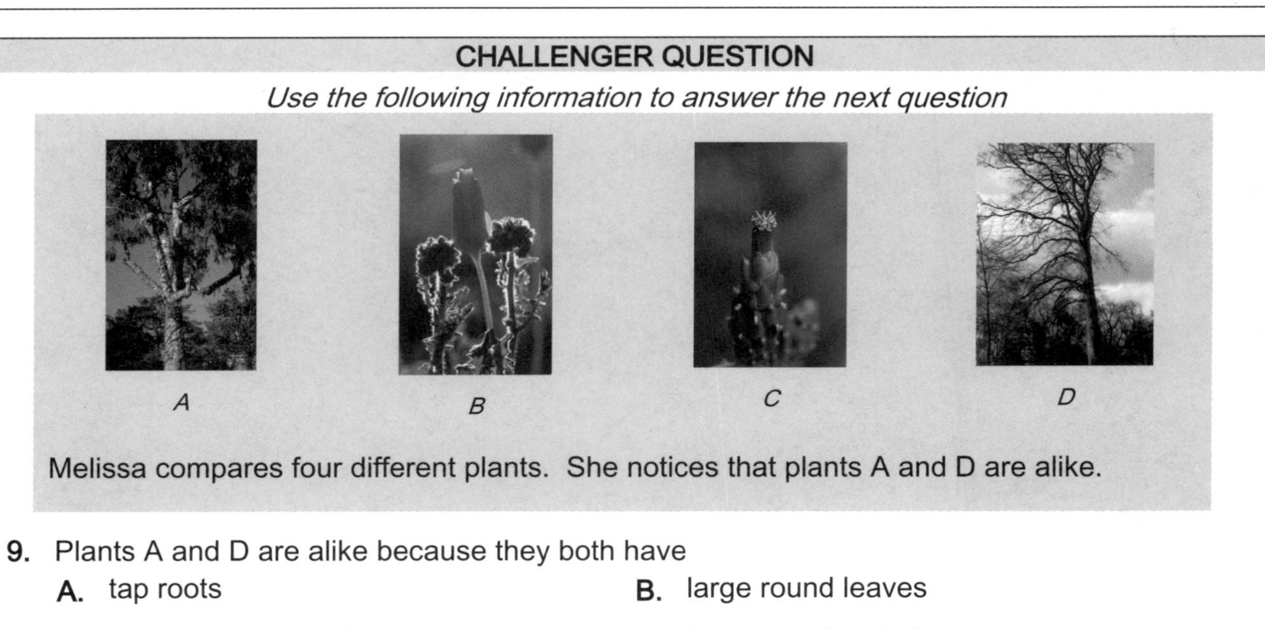

Melissa compares four different plants. She notices that plants A and D are alike.

9. Plants A and D are alike because they both have

   A. tap roots
   B. large round leaves
   C. a pistil and stamen
   D. bark covering their stems

Use the following information to answer the next question

Dennis is looking at a radish plant.

Radish

10. He knows that the radish stores its food energy in its

A. root **B.** stem **C.** seeds **D.** leaves

3LS2.3 *germinate seeds and record similarities and differences as seedlings develop*

3LS3.3 *describe the changes that different plants undergo in their life cycles*

THE LIFE CYCLE OF THE PLANT

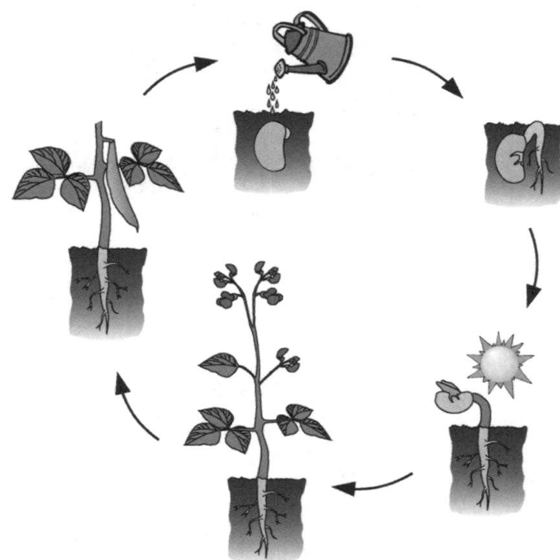

The life cycle of a bean plant

Many plants begin their lives as a seed. The seed needs to be in a warm place or in the ground. It begins to **germinate** or sprout. The seed grows in two directions. One part travels down into the soil to become the roots. The other part grows up to become the stem and leaves.

When it is big enough, the plant flowers. The flowers have pollen. The pollen is moved from flower to flower by insects or the wind. Once a flower has been pollinated, it begins to make seeds.

The petals fall off, and the flower begins to turn into fruit. The fruit contains the seeds. The seeds may be caught by the wind or carried away by animals. If they are planted or find a nice warm spot, the cycle begins again.

A dandelion's seeds catch the wind and fly far away from the parent plant.

Some plants also send out special roots or suckers under the ground. A new plant can grow from them. They stay attached to the parent plant. The trembling aspen is a tree that grows this way. They also produce seeds to make new plants far away from the parent plant.

An aspen forest often comes from only one plant.

Some plants can grow young plants from both seeds and underground bulbs. A bulb is a rounded underground stem. Within the bulb, special leaves store food for next year's growth. As they grow, new bulbs are formed. New plants can grow from the new bulbs the next year. An onion is an example of a bulb.

The onion's bulb has the food it needs to grow in the spring before it gets its leaves.

Bulb plants such as lilies can grow from seeds as well as a bulb. The seeds usually take a year to grow into a plant that has a bulb. It is faster to grow the plants from bulbs than from seeds.

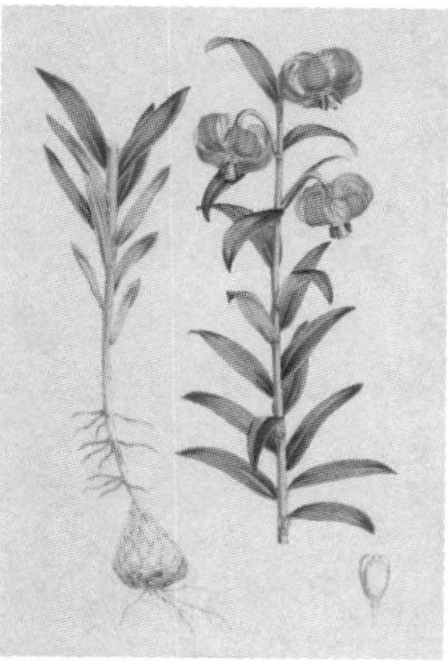

A lily makes new bulbs underground or seeds to grow new plants.

Practice

CHALLENGER QUESTION

Use the following information to answer the next question

The diagram shows the different growing stages of a seed plant. The stages are not necessarily in the correct order.

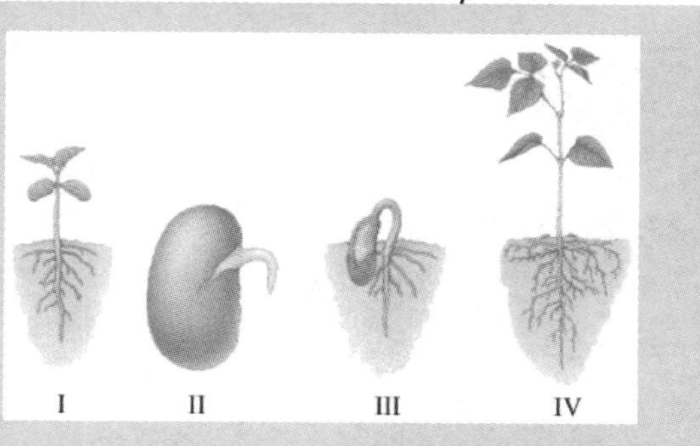

11. Which of the following lists has the stages of a seed plant listed in the **correct** order?

A. I → II → III → IV

B. III → IV → I → II

C. II → III → I → IV

D. IV → I → III → II

Use the following information to answer the next question

Evan volunteered to help in the wilderness park. He saw these seeds fall from a plant.

12. Which of the following plants will these seeds become?

A. 

B. 

C. 

D. 

13. When a seed begins to germinate, or sprout, it grows

A. only toward the ground

B. only toward the surface

C. both toward the ground and toward the surface

D. toward the ground, to the surface, and to the side

3LS3.4 *describe how most plants get energy to live directly from the sun and how plants help other living things to get energy from the sun*

Plants Use Energy from the Sun

All living things need energy to live. People and other animals get energy from eating food. You need energy to grow, run, laugh, and play. Plants need energy too. Plants get their energy from the sun. Plants do not need to run and play, but they do need to grow and produce offspring.

Plants can make their own food. Their leaves take in carbon dioxide gas from the air. They take in water and mineral nutrients from the soil. They use the energy from the sun to turn the carbon dioxide and water into food. This is called **photosynthesis**. Not all the energy a plant makes is used. Some of the energy is stored.

Animals can not make their own food from sunlight. They have to eat plants or other animals that eat plants. The energy that is stored in the plant is used by the animal that eats it. This moves the energy of the plant to the animal. Animals do not use all the food energy they take in. Some of the energy is stored in the animal's body.

Some animals eat only plants. Some animals eat other animals. The energy stored in the first animal is used by the animal that eats it. This moves the energy of the first animal to the second animal. These animals do not use all the energy they take in. Some of the energy is stored in their body.

Eventually, these animals die. Animals called **scavengers** eat the dead animals. They use the stored food energy next. In this way, the energy from the sun is passed from plant to animal to animal.

The movement of energy from one living thing to another can be shown in a **food chain**. The food chain uses arrows to show the direction that the sun's energy moves. The arrows point to the living thing receiving the energy.

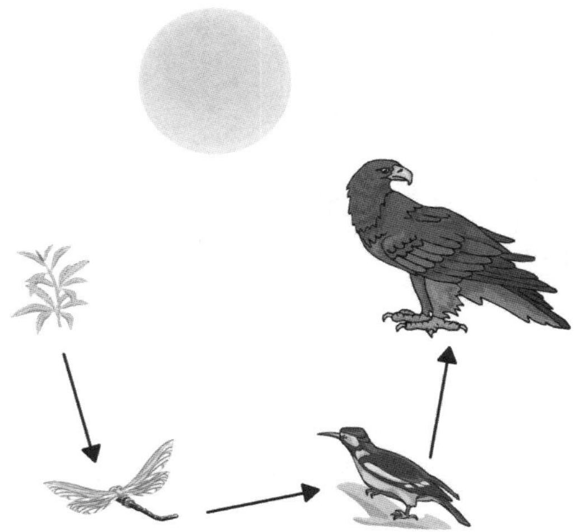

The energy from the sun moves from the plants to each of the animals in this food chain.

Practice

14. Plants use energy from the sun to

A. turn sunlight into water

B. turn water into carbon dioxide

C. turn carbon dioxide and water into food

D. turn sunlight into carbon dioxide and food

CHALLENGER QUESTION

Use the following information to answer the next question

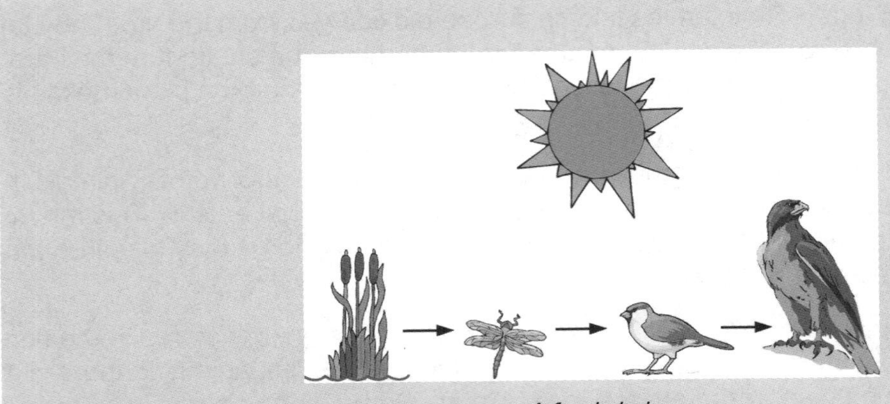

A food chain

15. This food chain shows how

A. heat is passed on to living things

B. energy from the sun is lost over time

C. energy is moved from one living thing to another

D. sunlight is absorbed by a variety of different animals

3LS3.5 *describe ways in which humans from various cultures, including Aboriginal people, use plants for food, shelter, medicine, and clothing*

Describing How People Use Plants

Plants are very useful. People around the world have been using plants for all sorts of purposes for a very long time.

Food

Humans have gathered fruit and nuts from plants for thousands of years. People dig up and eat the roots or tubers of many plants such as carrots and potatoes. Eventually, people learned that they could plant the crops they wanted in one place and farming began. Farms can grow wheat, canola, rice, squash, apples, and many more crops. Plants are a very important source of food.

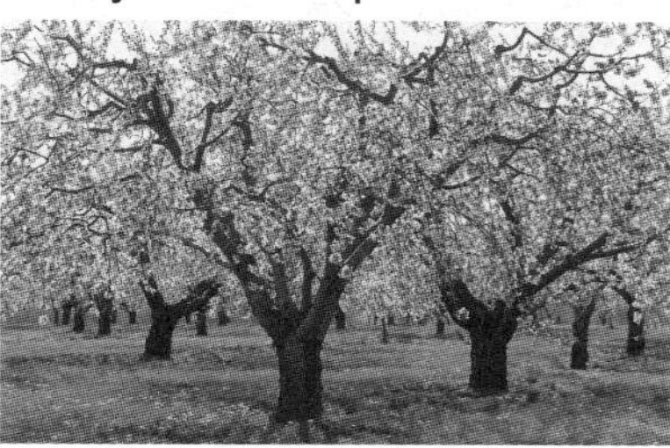

An apple orchard is a farm where apples are grown.

Shelter

Trees are used to build homes. In the past, the Iroquois built longhouses. They made a frame from wooden poles and covered it in bark. In modern times, many homes are still made from a wood frame. Your house may be made of wood.

A house is being built from wood.

In Asia, many traditional homes were made from bamboo. Even today, bamboo is still used as a building material. It is as strong as steel but much less expensive. Bamboo is tall and sturdy like a tree, but it is in the grass family. It grows faster than trees. It takes many years for a forest of trees to grow back. A bamboo forest can grow back in only three years.

MEDICINE

Many medicines are made from plants. Ingredients in some pain relievers and cough medicines come from plants. Aboriginal peoples used plants for medicine. The sap of pine trees was used on cuts to stop infection. Teas made from plants were used for upset stomach.

The needles of the Eastern white pine are high in vitamin C. They were used to treat a disease called scurvy.

CLOTHING

Cotton comes from the fluffy top of a cotton plant. It is called a boll. It is collected and spun into thread to make clothes. For centuries, cotton has been used around the world to make clothes.Flax is a plant used to make a fabric called linen. Fibres from the stem are used. They are also spun into thread. Even bamboo fibres are now used to make clothing.

A cotton plant with bolls

Practice

Use the following information to answer the next question

16. Humans from many cultures around the world use plants like these as an important source of

    A. food
    B. heat for homes
    C. plastic materials
    D. shelter materials

Use the following information to answer the next question

The First Nations people have used plants for many things. For example, they have used sap from trees to stop cuts from becoming infected. They have also used plants in tea to help treat an upset stomach.

17. These uses show how plants are valuable as

    A. food
    B. shelter
    C. clothing
    D. medicine

3LS3.6 *describe ways in which plants and animals depend on each other*

Plants and Animals Depend on Each Other

Plants are a source of food for many animals. Many kinds of insects eat the leaves of plants. Some drink the nectar from the flowers. Some kinds of animals, such as deer and rabbits, eat only plants. Some birds eat the seeds or fruit of plants.

Animals can help plants make more plants. As an insect moves around inside a flower getting nectar, they get pollen on their bodies. When they fly to another flower, the pollen brushes onto the second flower. The flower needs the pollen to make seeds. Insects help flowers make seeds.

Insects help flowers make seeds.

Many animals like to eat fruit. Birds like to eat fruit such as berries. The seeds in the fruit pass through the bird's digestive system. The seeds then get scattered far away from the parent plant.

Humans and animals need air to breathe. People need the oxygen in the air. People breathe it in and breathe out carbon dioxide. Plants need carbon dioxide. They take carbon dioxide from the air. They release oxygen into the air. Plants make the oxygen that people and animals need to breathe. You could not breathe without plants. Plants use the carbon dioxide from people and animals to make food.

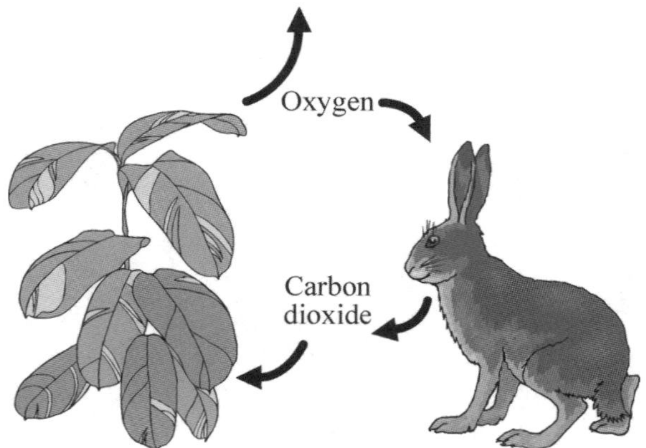

Plants give off oxygen, and animals breathe in oxygen.

Plants give some animals a place to live or a place to hide. Many animals make their home in trees. Many birds make nests high up in trees. Some kinds of insects attach their cocoons or lay their eggs on plants. Some insects look like the plant they live on. This helps them hide from other animals that want to eat them.

18. Animals help plants by

- **A.** giving them food
- **B.** making clean soil
- **C.** breathing out oxygen
- **D.** breathing out carbon dioxide

CHALLENGER QUESTION

Use the following information to answer the next question

19. This type of insect lives on or close to plants. It is safe for this insect to stay where it is because it

- **A.** looks like the plant it lives on
- **B.** can eat the same plant for many years
- **C.** helps the plant attract bees to spread pollen
- **D.** attracts a lot of attention by staying on the plant

3LS3.7 *describe the different ways in which plants are grown for food, and explain the advantages and disadvantages of locally grown and organically produced food, including environmental benefits*

The Different Ways Food is Grown

Machinery harvests the food.

Most human food is grown on farms. A farm is a large area of land where crops are planted. Some farms grow only one type of crop. Other farms grow a few different crops. The plants are planted in long rows. The rows make it easy to plant and care for the crops.

The trees in an orchard are planted in neat rows.

Fruit is sometimes grown in an orchard. An orchard is a farm where fruit trees are planted in neat rows. Apples, peaches, and pears are grown this way.

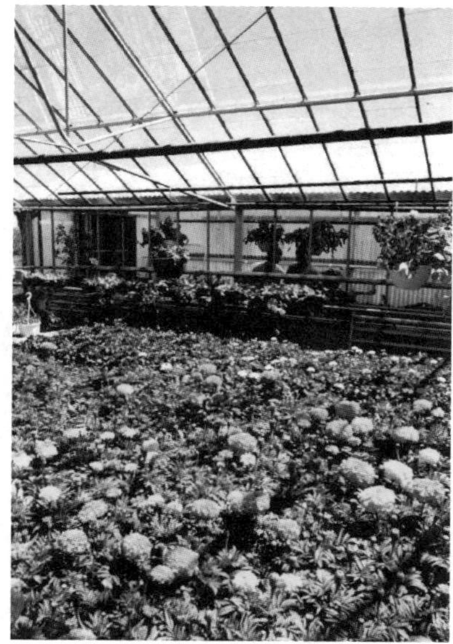

The ceiling and walls of a greenhouse are windows.

Some food is grown in a greenhouse. A greenhouse is a building for growing plants. The walls and ceiling of a greenhouse are made of windows. The windows let in a lot of light. A greenhouse is warm inside. The air is very moist.

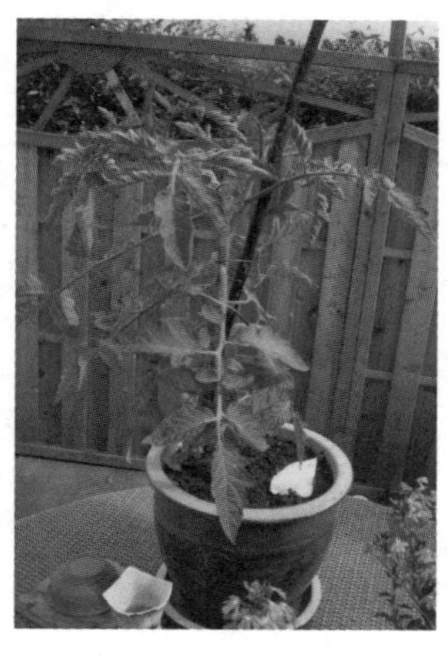

Vegetables can be grown in small pots on a balcony.

Many people grow food at home. Some have gardens in their backyard. Some grow tomatoes or strawberries in pots on their balcony. Some apartment buildings have community gardens on their rooftop.

Organically and Locally Grown Foods

Many people choose to buy fruits and vegetables that have been **organically grown**. Organically grown food does not have chemical fertilizers or pesticides added to them.

Here are some of the good things about *organically grown* food:

- Organically grown food does not use pesticides. Many people are concerned about pesticides. Pesticides are chemicals that kill insects and weeds. Without pesticides, the insects might eat the plants. The weeds might take mineral nutrients from the crops. But pesticides are harmful to the environment. They can also be harmful to people.
- Organically grown food uses natural fertilizer like compost. Fertilizer puts important mineral nutrients in the soil. It helps plants grow. Natural fertilizer is better for the soil.

Here are some of the problems of organically grown food:

- Organically grown food costs more money than other kinds of food. Many people can not afford to buy it.
- Organic farms are small, and there are not many of them. At this time, there is not enough organically grown food for everyone.

Do you live in a town or a city? If you do, you probably buy your groceries from a grocery store. Many of the fruits and vegetables in your grocery store have come from far away places. They flew to Canada on an airplane from places like New Zealand, Chile, or Argentina. Many people feel it is important to buy fruits and vegetables from farmers in or near their own community. Food that grows in or near your community is **locally grown**.

Here are some of the good things about locally grown food:

- Buying food that was grown closer to your home is better for the environment. Airplanes use a lot of energy and pollute the air. When the food does not have to travel so far, fewer fossil fuels are used. There is also less air pollution.
- Locally grown food does not need chemicals to keep it fresh. Certain chemicals are used to keep the food fresh on its long journey. If the food is grown in or near your community, these chemicals do not need to be used.

Here are some of the problems of locally grown food:

- Places with cold climates, such as the territories in Northern Canada, cannot grow many things. They must get fresh fruits and vegetables from other places.
- Only certain kinds of food can be grown locally. Bananas, for example, cannot grow in Canada.
- If the weather is bad one year and crops are lost, there could be food shortages.

Practice

Use the following information to answer the next question

There are certain crops that farmers in Ontario can not grow. The growing season is not as long as it is in other parts of the world. It does not get as hot in the summer as it does in the tropics.

20. This disadvantage to growing local crops means that

A. farmers must move to warmer places

B. food must be imported from other places

C. people cannot buy food that is grown in other areas of the world

D. soil must be changed so that all crops from around the world can grow in it

Use the following information to answer the next question

Many people choose to buy fruits and vegetables that have been organically grown.

21. An advantage to buying organically grown food is that

A. it costs less to buy

B. organically grown food does not use pesticides

C. organically grown plants require new soil each time

D. there are many organic farms that can supply everyone with organic food

3LS3.8 *identify examples of environmental conditions that may threaten plant and animal survival*

Threats to Plants and Animals

Plants and animals face many threats. Some come from nature and some from people.

Weather

In Canada, it is usually cold in the winter and warm in the summer. Most plants and animals can live through normal weather. They have adaptations to help them. An **adaptation** is something a plant or animal has or does that helps it survive. Some animals may grow extra fur to stay warm. Some plants have a thick, waxy covering so they do not lose water on a hot day. But sometimes, the weather is very harsh. If it is too hot or too cold, some plants and animals will die.

Plants and animals can die during very cold winters.

They can also die if there is too much or not enough rain. Too much rain can cause flooding. Floods can uproot or wash away plants or trees.

A drought is a long period of time with little or no rain. Plants and animals cannot live without water. Many plants can die during a drought.

But this is all part of nature. These cycles are important. They keep plant and animal populations from getting too big.

PEOPLE

People can be a threat to plants and animals too. People clear land to build cities and farms. Plants and animals lose their homes. With no safe place to live, they may die.

Motorized personal watercraft can be dangerous for wildlife. Many birds make nests in the plants along the shore. The noise from the motors can scare the birds away from their nests. This leaves the nest unprotected.

A boat makes a trail of waves in the water behind it. These waves can flood a nest. The eggs may be lost. Boats and other watercraft may leave oily materials behind. These materials float on the water and may harm plants and animals.

Plants can be damaged too. Water plants can get caught in the boat's motor. Some kinds of personal watercraft shoot jets of water out the back. The water jets are powerful. They can damage the plants.

Motorized personal watercraft can damage the nests of shorebirds.

Use the following information to answer the next question

A construction company plans on building a new mall next to a town. The mall will be built where a local forest now stands.

22. The **most likely** effect of building the new mall is that
   - **A.** the plants will receive more sunlight, reflecting off the windows of the stores
   - **B.** more plants will grow because of the extra water being used by the mall
   - **C.** more plants will grow from all the extra carbon dioxide
   - **D.** the plants in the forest will be cleared away

Use the following information to answer the next question

Using gas-powered watercraft on lakes is a popular activity in the summer months in Canada.

23. These watercraft may cause problems for water plants because

A. they need a large amount of water to work

B. they attract many animals that eat water plants

C. the powerful water jets that shoot out of watercraft can damage the plants

D. the speed of the boats causes a very fast current that washes plants away

3LS2.1 *follow established safety procedures during science and technology investigations*

Safety Rules

During this unit, you may do experiments on plants. Here are some safety rules to remember:

- Plants are a source of food for people and animals. But some plants or plant parts are poisonous. They can make you sick. Only taste plants that a teacher or adult has given you permission to eat.
- Some people are allergic to some plants. It is important to tell your teacher if you have any plant allergies.
- Remember to wash your hands after handling plants and soil.

Practice

24. You should never taste a plant without permission from an adult because it

A. may be poisonous

B. may be too big to eat

C. needs to have rotten parts removed

D. has seeds that need to be replanted first

3LS2.4 *investigate ways in which a variety of plants adapt and/or react to their environment, including changes in their environment, using a variety of methods*

Plant Adaptations

Plants grow and live all over the world. Some plants can live anywhere. Some are only found in certain places. Plants have adaptations to help meet their needs. These adaptations help them to survive.

An *adaptation* is something that a plant has or does to help it survive. For example, many plants follow the sun with their leaves or flowers. This adaptation lets the plant collect as much sunlight as possible.

Adaptations can change over time. These changes usually happen because the environment changes. Plants that can adapt to changes will survive. Those that cannot may not survive.

A cactus is a plant that has many adaptations. It has a thick, waxy coating. This helps keep water in the plant. A cactus also has long roots that grow just under the surface of the earth. The long roots can collect a lot of water from the ground when it rains.

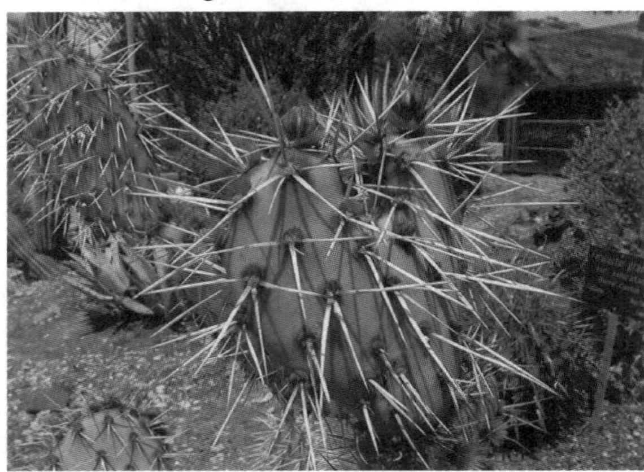

Cactus roots let the plant take in water quickly.

Plants that grow in forests will grow tall and thin to get closer to the sunlight. Other plants in the same area may grow better in shaded spots. They have adapted to growing near the base of trees.

Shade-loving plants live on the forest floor.

Some plants have brightly colored flowers to attract bees and other insects. Some plants give off a scent that attracts insects. The insects help to spread pollen to other plants. This helps more plants grow.

Insects are attracted to brightly coloured flowers.

Plants have many different ways of sending out their seeds. New plants can get a good start by growing away from the parent plant. There will be more room to grow. They will not have to compete with the parent plant for water and mineral nutrients.

Wind blows dandelion seeds away from the flower. Dandelion seeds have hair-like parts attached to a stalk. The seeds are carried like a parachute caught in the wind. Other seeds are carried away by water. Some have hooks or barbs that stick to the fur of animals. This pushes the seeds far from the parent plant.

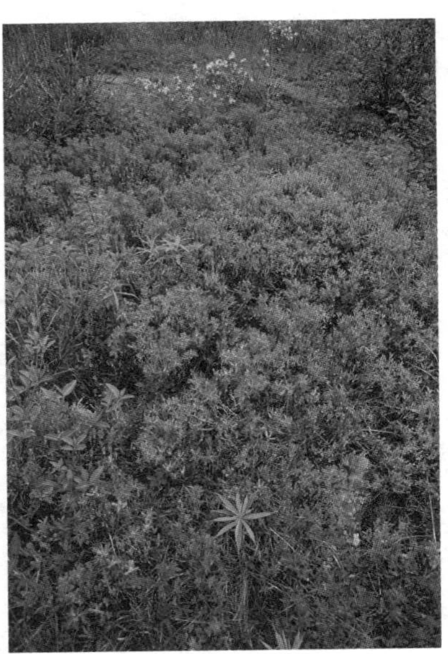

Labrador tea grows in bogs.

Some plants, such as the Labrador tea, have adapted to living in places that have poor soil. The Labrador tea lives in bogs. It cannot get all the mineral nutrients (chemicals) it needs from the soil. A fungus lives around the roots of the plant. The fungus changes chemicals in the soil so the plant can use them. The plant provides some food for the fungus too.

Practice

25. Which of the following plants has an adaptation to survive in the desert?

A. 

B. 

C. 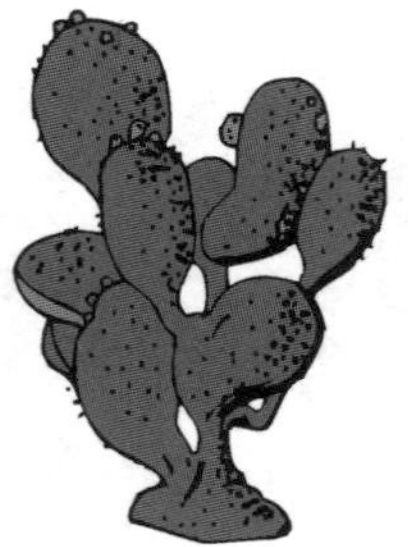

D. 

26. Flowers often have brightly colored petals in order to

A. make food

B. catch sunlight

C. attract insects and birds

D. scare away insects and birds

3LS2.6 *use appropriate science and technology vocabulary, including stem, leaf, root, pistil, stamen, flower, adaptation, and germination, in oral and written communication*

VOCABULARY

Please look in the glossary to find the following vocabulary words: **stem**, **leaf**, **root**, **pistil**, **stamen**, **flower**, **adaptation**, and **germination**.

27. Which part of the plant moves water and minerals to all parts of the plant?

A. Leaf　**B.** Pistil　**C.** Stem　**D.** Flower

SOLUTIONS—LIFE SYSTEMS: GROWTH AND CHANGES IN PLANTS

1. D	7. C	13. C	19. A	25. C
2. C	8. B	14. C	20. B	26. C
3. A	9. D	15. C	21. B	27. C
4. D	10. A	16. A	22. D	
5. D	11. C	17. D	23. C	
6. C	12. D	18. D	24. A	

1. D
Trees provide humans with lumber to build structures like buildings or even boats.

2. C
This city park most likely helps to lower the carbon dioxide levels in the city. Plants use carbon dioxide to make oxygen.

3. A
Houseplants are good for you because they can clean the air inside your home.

4. D
Non-native plants could escape the garden and spread throughout the area. Since non-native plants may not have any predators, they can spread easily. This could choke out any native plants too.

5. D
The roots of a plant bring up minerals from the soil. Minerals help the plant to grow.

6. C
Julie's plant died because it did not get any sunlight. Plants need light to make their food.

7. C
Plants on mountains grow low to the ground to stay warm. These areas often have very cold winds. In the summer, the sun warms the earth. Plants that are low to the ground are closer to the heated earth. Plants need to stay warm to survive and grow.

8. B
The pistil is shown by arrow 2.

9. D
Plants A and D are both trees. Trees have hard stems that are covered in bark. Each year a tree lives, a new layer is added to the stem.

10. A
A radish stores its food energy in its root.

11. C
The correct order of the stages of a seed plant is II → III → I → IV. The seed plant starts as a seed (II). When it sprouts, parts will grow down into the earth to form the roots (III). Other parts will grow upward to form the stem and leaves (I). The seedling or sprout will grow bigger into an adult plant (IV).

12. D
As these seed grow in their life cycle, they will grow up to look much like their parent plant. This is best shown by picture D.

13. C
The seed grows in two directions. One part travels down into the soil to become the roots. The other part grows up to become the stem and leaves.

14. C
Plants turn carbon dioxide and water into food. They need energy from the sun to do this.

15. C
Food chains show the movement of energy from one living thing to another. The food chain uses arrows to show the direction that the sun's energy moves. The arrows point to the living thing receiving the energy.

16. A
Fruits and vegetables are a very important source of food.

17. D
Plants are valuable for medicines. Ingredients in some pain relievers come from plants. Plants have been used for medicine by First Nations people.

18. D

Animals breathe out carbon dioxide. Plants use the carbon dioxide to make their food. During this process, plants release oxygen to the air, which animals need.

19. A

This insect looks like the plant it lives on. This can help protect it from other animals that might want to eat it.

20. B

Food must be imported from other places. This adds to the variety of food grown locally. The climate in Canada can be very harsh. Farmers cannot grow food such as bananas because of this.

21. B

Organically grown food does not use pesticides. Pesticides are chemicals that kill insects and weeds. They can also be harmful to people.

22. D

The plants in the forest would most likely have to be cleared away to construct the mall. People clear land to build cities and farms, and this can harm the local plant life.

23. C

Personal watercraft have very powerful water jets that shoot out of the back. This can damage water plants because of how strong the jets are.

24. A

Some plants or plant parts are poisonous. They can make you sick. Only taste plants that a teacher or adult has given you permission to eat.

25. C

Cactus plants have broad, fleshy stems. This adaptation helps them to store water. They also have long, shallow roots that soak up water quickly in hot areas.

26. C

Flowers are brightly colored and scented to attract insects and small birds. These animals pick up the flower's pollen on their bodies, which they carry to another plant when they travel.

27. C

The stem of a plant has tubes that move water and minerals. The water and minerals move up from the roots to all the parts of the plant. The stem also holds the plant up to the sunlight.

NOTES

Unit Test

Use the following information to answer the next question

The city shown has tall buildings. Some are for offices, and others are for apartments.

1. These buildings have a positive effect on plant habitats because
   A. they hold soil in place for plants to grow
   B. less land is needed to construct new buildings
   C. sunlight is reflected toward forests from tall buildings
   D. they block very strong winds from reaching plant habitats

Use the following information to answer the next question

Laura wants to beautify a nature park outside her city. She wants to try to protect the plants at the same time. Many people travel there to see the plants and wildlife.

2. Which of the following actions allows Laura to beautify and protect the park?
   A. Making a new hiking trail in the park
   B. Planting native species of plants in the trail areas
   C. Planting new non-native plants that are very colourful
   D. Picking the blossoms of one type of wildflower to show tourists

3. A plant kept in a dark closet will die because
   A. plants need oxygen to grow
   B. plants need sunlight to grow
   C. the closet will fill up with too much oxygen
   D. the closet will fill up with too much carbon dioxide

Use the following information to answer the next question

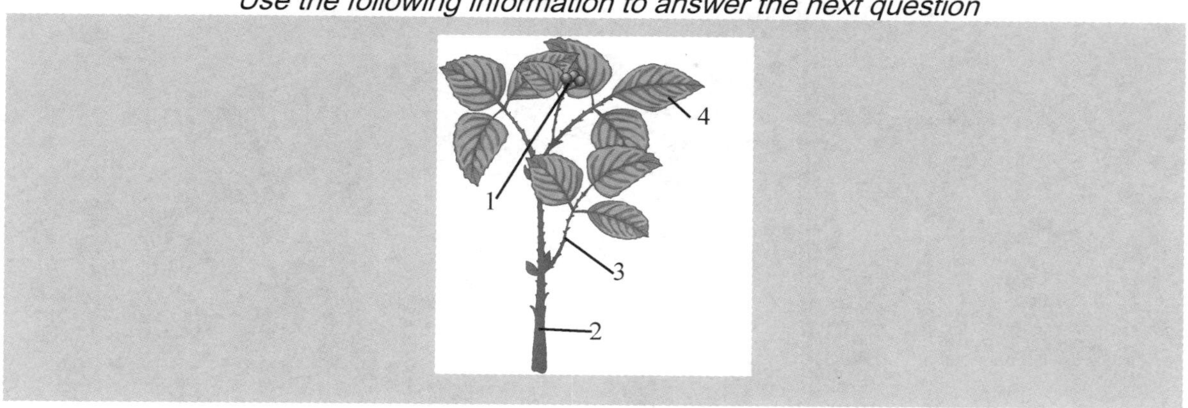

4. The part of this plant that takes in sunshine and carbon dioxide gas from the air is labelled

   A. 1 B. 2 C. 3 D. 4

Use the following information to answer the next question

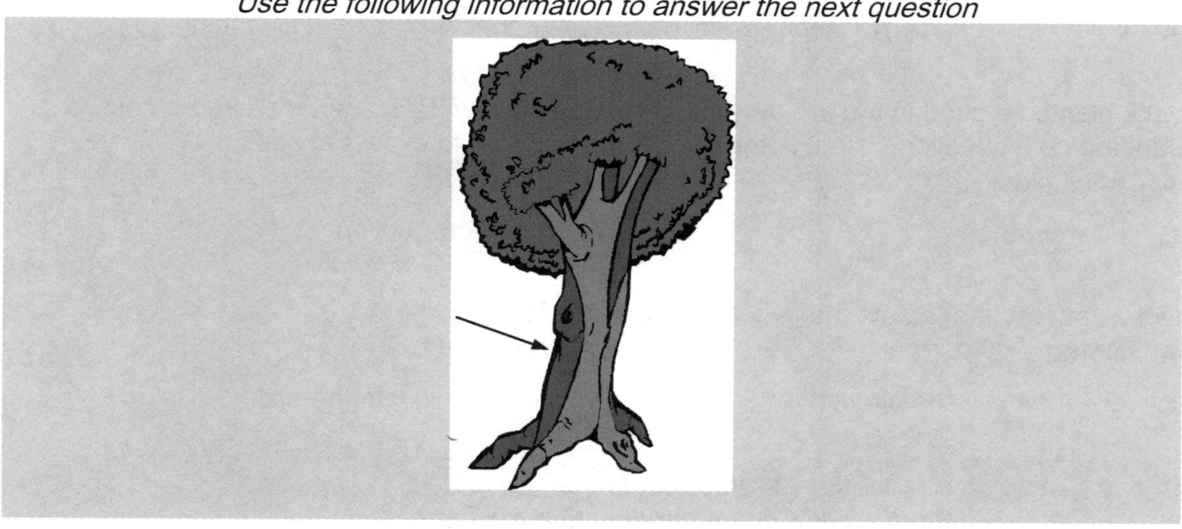

5. The part of the tree the arrow is pointing to is called the

   A. fruit B. stem C. roots D. leaves

Use the following information to answer the next question

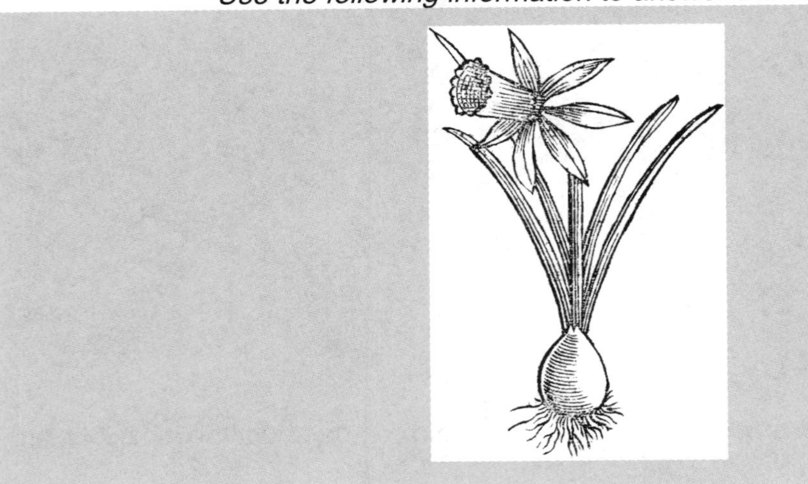

6. This plant grows from a
   A. bulb B. seed C. runner D. cutting

7. Jack planted a seed in the ground and watered it. A few days later, the seed sprouted, sending up a seedling. What is the next stage Jack could expect to see?
   A. Adult plant
   B. Fruit stage
   C. Flower stage
   D. Seed production

8. Not all energy that plants make is used. Some of the energy is
   A. stored
   B. recycled
   C. given off into the air
   D. sent down into the soil

CHALLENGER QUESTION

Use the following information to answer the next question

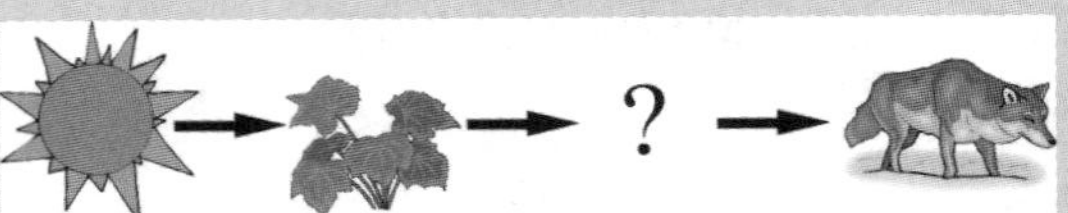

This diagram shows how energy from the sun is passed on from plants to animals.

9. Which of the following animals **best** fits into the missing spot?
   A. Eagle B. Seal C. Bear D. Deer

10. Which of the following items was **most likely** made using cotton plants?

A. 

B. 

C. 

D. 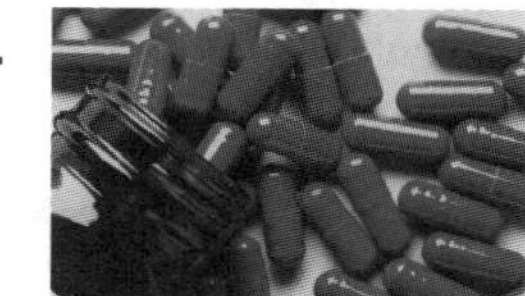

11. Which of the following statements **best** describes how birds and plants depend on each other?

A. Birds like to eat berries made by plants and spread the seeds to other places.

B. Birds live inside plants, and the plants need the heat that birds provide.

C. Birds like to use the bright colours of flowers to attract other birds.

D. Birds dig up the bulbs of plants and move them to new places.

Use the following information to answer the next question

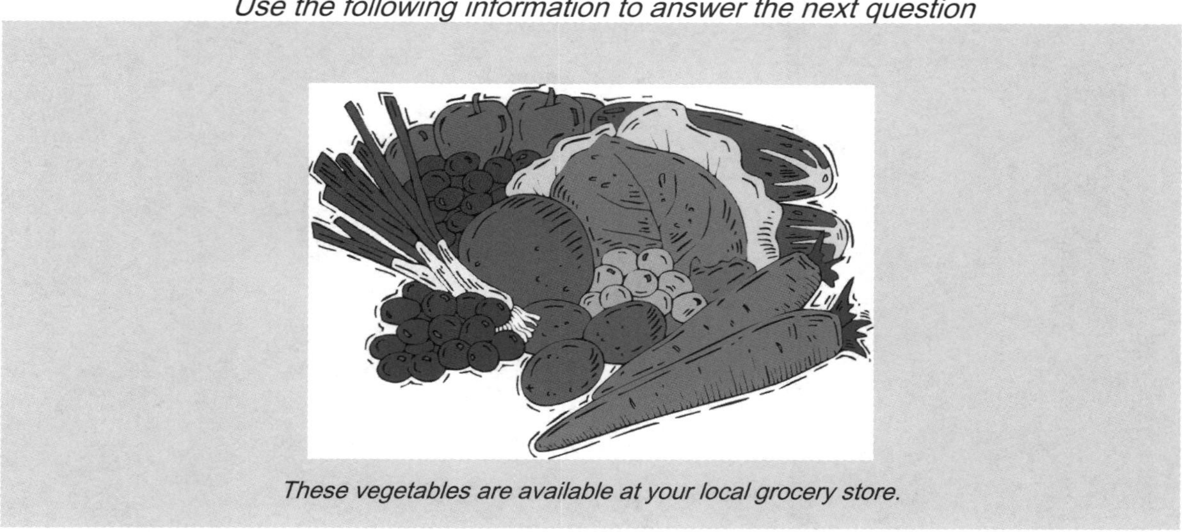

These vegetables are available at your local grocery store.

12. Where are these vegetables **mainly** grown?

A. Orchards B. Marshes C. Forests D. Farms

13. Which of the following areas does **not** allow plants to live because of very little water?

A. 

B. 

C. 

D. 

14. Some people are allergic to plants. Which of the following pictures **best** shows the action to take after handling plants?

A. 

B. 

C. 

D. 

Use the following information to answer the next question

Plants have many different types of leaves. The type of leaf depends on the particular plant.

15. Which of the following leaves stays green the entire year?

A. 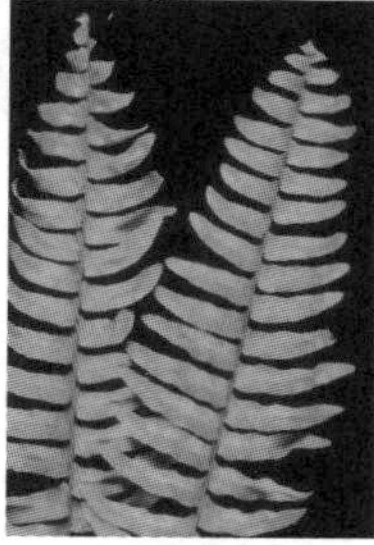

B. 

C. 

D. 

16. If a plant starts its life cycle as a seed, then it ends its life cycles as a

A. fruit **B.** bulb **C.** flower **D.** seedling

17. Some desert plants have a waxy covering on their leaves to

A. attract insects

B. stop them from losing water

C. protect the plants from enemies

D. allow them to stay green in the heat

CHALLENGER QUESTION

Use the following information to answer the next question

Joan has to water four different plants. Joan wants to know how often she should water each plant. She has decided to test the plants by allowing them to almost dry out between waterings. Her results are recorded in the table.

Plant	Number of Days for Soil to Almost Dry Out
Ivy	4
Cactus	6
Violet	7
Fern	5

18. The plant that uses the **greatest** amount of water is the
    A. ivy B. fern C. violet D. cactus

Use the following information to answer the next question

When Dallas went to visit his aunt, he found this plant outside in the backyard.

19. Dallas noticed that the plant **most likely** needed
    A. more sunlight
    B. a smaller pot
    C. some water
    D. fresh air

20. Which part of a plant takes in water and chemicals from the soil?
    A. Flower B. Roots C. Stem D. Leaf

Solutions

1. B	5. B	9. D	13. D	17. B
2. B	6. A	10. A	14. A	18. A
3. B	7. A	11. A	15. D	19. C
4. D	8. A	12. D	16. A	20. B

1. B

People need space to live. Cities often make space for houses by clearing habitats used by plants and animals. Taller buildings save on space by building up instead of out.

2. B

Laura should plant only native plants in the trail areas. Planting a non-native species is not a good idea because it could spread. The non-native plants will take over an area that native plants used to live on.

3. B

A plant kept in a dark closet will die because plants need sunlight to grow.

4. D

The part labelled 4 is a leaf. Leaves take in light from the sun and carbon dioxide gas from the air. They are used to make food for the plant.

5. B

The arrow is pointing to the stem. The stem of a tree is very hard and is covered in bark.

6. A

This plant grows from a bulb. As this plant grows, new bulbs are formed. New plants can grow from the new bulbs the next year.

7. A

The next stage after the seedling stage is the adult plant. The adult forms a flower and then a fruit. The fruit produces seeds. This will start the cycle again.

8. A

Any energy the plant does not use is stored. This stored energy may be used by an animal that eats the plant.

9. D

A wolf eats a deer for energy. The deer gets its energy from eating a plant. The plant has stored energy from the sun. This is how energy from the sun is passed on from plants to animals.

10. A

The sweater was most likely made using cotton from cotton plants. For centuries, cotton has been used around the world to make clothes.

11. A

Birds like to eat fruit such as berries. The seeds in the fruit pass through the bird's digestive system. The seeds then get scattered far away from the parent plant.

12. D

Fruit and vegetables are mainly grown on farms. A farm is a large area of land where crops are planted. Some farms grow only one type of crop. Other farms grow a few different crops.

13. D

This picture shows an area that is experiencing a drought. A drought is caused by little or no rain and can kill many plants.

14. A

After handling plants, you should always wash your hands. This will protect other people who may be allergic to the plants you have handled. You should never rub your eyes or eat without washing your hands.

15. D

Pine trees have needles for leaves. They stay green all year.

16. A

A plant that starts from a seed will end its life cycle as a fruit. The fruit contains the seeds, which eventually reach the ground. The life cycle then starts again.

17. B

Desert plants have a thick, waxy covering on their leaves to stop them from losing water. The waxy coating keeps the water inside their leaves.

18. A

Since the ivy dried out the fastest, it needed the most water. All plants need water to survive.

19. C

This plant needs more water. When plants do not get enough water, they wilt or droop.

20. B

The roots take in water and chemicals from the soil. Some plants have roots that store sugar. The sugar is food for the plant. Roots also hold the plant in the ground.

Strong and Stable Structures

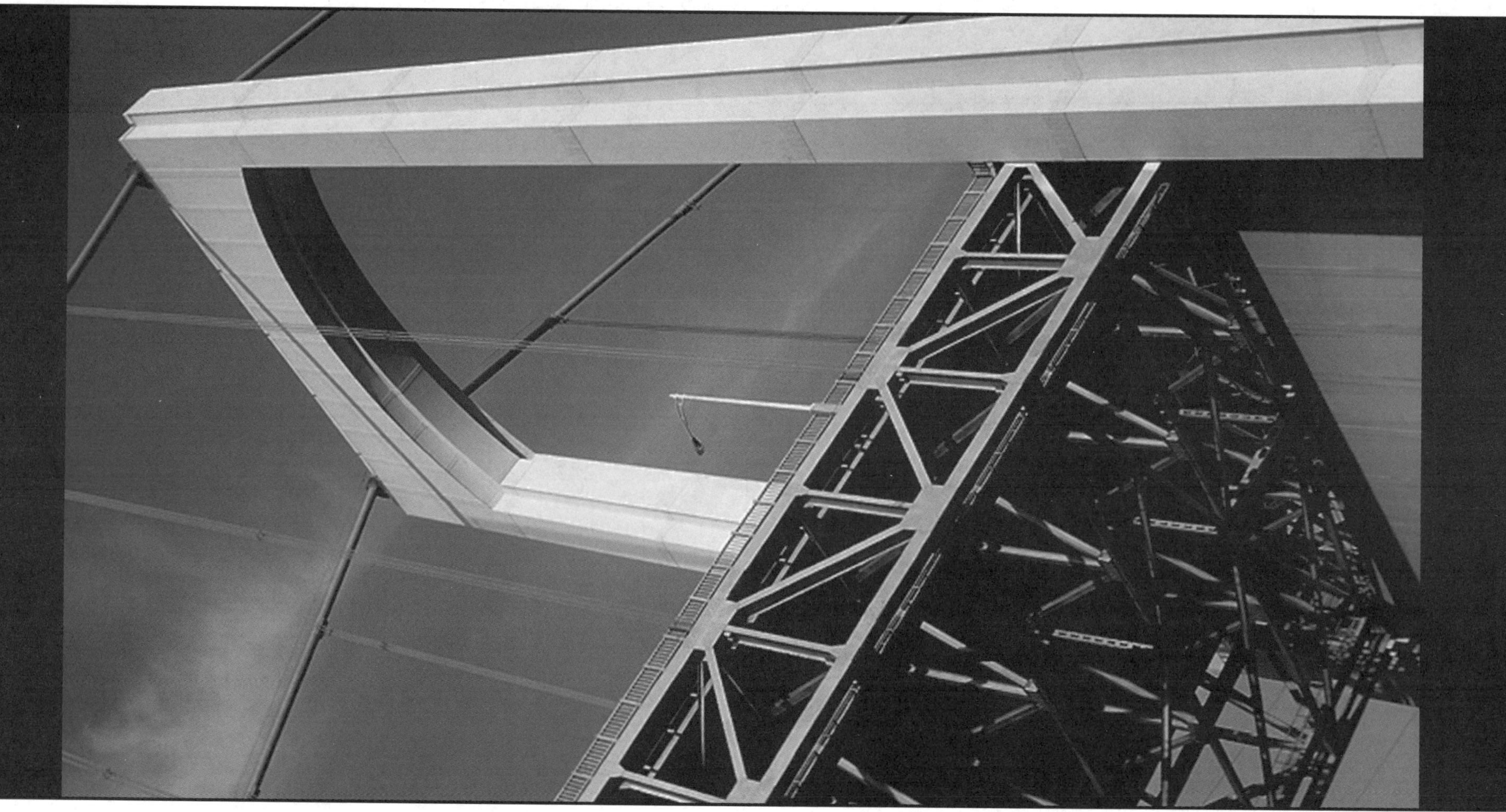

Structures and Mechanisms: Strong and Stable Structures

Table of Correlations

	Specific Expectation	Practice Questions	Unit Test Questions
3SM1:STSE	Assess the importance of form, function, strenght, and stability in structures through time;		
3SM1.1	*assess effects of strong and stable structures on society and the environment*	1, 2	1
3SM1.2	*assess the environmental impact of structures built by various animals and those built by humans*	3, 4	2, 3
3SM3:Concepts	Demonstrate an understanding of the concepts of structure, strength, and stability and the factors that affect them.		
3SM3.1	*define a structure as a supporting framework, with a definite size, shape, and purpose, that holds a load*	5	4
3SM3.2	*identify structures in the natural environment and in the built environment*	6, 7	5
3SM3.3	*identify the strength of a structure as its ability to support a load*	8	6
3SM3.4	*identify the stability of a structure as its ability to maintain balance and stay fixed in one spot*	9	7
3SM3.5	*identify properties of materials that need to be considered when building structures*	10, 11	8
3SM3.6	*describe ways in which the strength of different materials can be altered*	12	9
3SM3.7	*describe ways to improve a structure's strength and stability*	15, 16	10
3SM3.8	*explain how strength and stability enable a structure to perform a specific function*	19, 20	11
3SM3.9	*describe ways in which different forces can affect the shape, balance, or position of structures*	21, 22	12, 13
3SM3.10	*identify the role of struts and ties in structures under load*	17	14
3SM2:Skills	Investigate strong and stable structures to determine how their design and materials enable them to perform their load-bearing function;		
3SM2.1	*follow established safety procedures during science and technology investigations*	23, 24	15
3SM2.2	*investigate, through experimentation, how various materials and construction techniques can be used to add strength to structures*	13, 14	16
3SM2.3	*investigate, through experimentation, the effects of pushing, pulling, and other forces on the shape and stability of simple structures*	18	17
3SM2.4	*use technological problem-solving skills, and knowledge acquired from previous investigations, to design and build a strong and stable structure that serves a purpose*	25, 26	18, 19
3SM2.5	*use appropriate science and technology vocabulary, including compression, tension, strut, ties, strength, and stability, in oral and written communication*	27	20

3SM1.1 *assess effects of strong and stable structures on society and the environment*

STRUCTURES IN THE WORLD AROUND YOU

Everywhere you look you can see structures. A **structure** holds a load and has a planned size, shape, and purpose. They can be big or small and have few parts or many parts. Some are found in nature, and others are made by humans. Structures are needed by both people and animals.

Structures are used by animals to help them get food and for shelter. Spiders make webs to gather food. Beavers build dams. The dam makes a deep pool where they can build their lodge. Birds build nests to raise their young. You can find beaver dams and birds' nests that have lasted for many years. Ants build anthills to live in, to raise their young, and to store food. Trees and mountains are natural structures too.

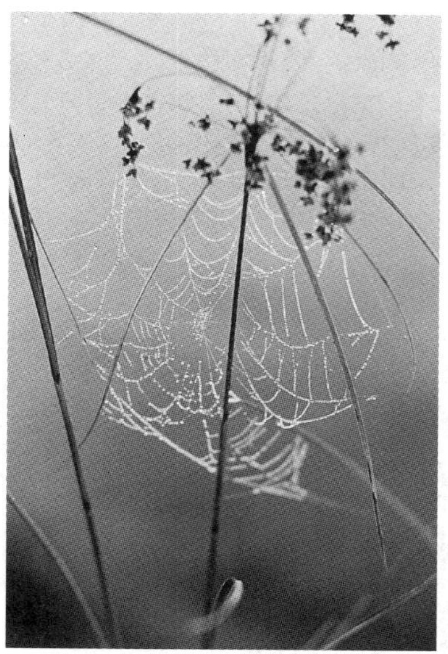

Spiders make webs to gather food.

People depend on structures. People make structures such as buildings, bicycles, airplanes, tables, and bridges. Structures are used for shelter, travel, and to make life easier.

This bridge is made of stone.

Buildings give people a safe place to live. Furniture gives a comfortable place to sit and work. People use bicycles and airplanes to get around from place to place. Bridges are used to cross rivers and streams. Some bridges now even let people cross large bodies of water such as the Northumberland Strait. The Northumberland Strait runs between Prince Edward Island and New Brunswick. Confederation Bridge crosses this strait and is nearly 13 kilometres long.

Structures need to be strong. Some of them last for a very long time. Some buildings are thousands of years old.

Scientists study these ancient structures to learn about the people that made them.

Some ancient structures were used for homes. Others were gathering places for many people. People learned which shapes were the strongest. They learned which materials were best. They learned how to use these materials. People often learned from noticing structures in nature.

When people no longer need the structures they have built, they stop using them. Sometimes, these structures fall down. Sometimes, they need to be removed to make room for new structures.

Many of the building materials can be recycled. Metal can be melted down and turned into new metal. Concrete can be crushed and used again. But some building materials cannot be recycled. They must be sent to a landfill.

Nature is able to get rid of its own structures. Nests and dams fall apart. Trees rot and turn into part of the soil. Mountains weather into small rocks. Nature recycles its structures.

Practice

Use the following information to answer the next question

Jake walked past 4 different fences on the way to school. Each fence was made of different materials.

1. Which fence will **most likely** last the longest?

A. 

B. 

C. 

D. 

2. Both people and animals use structures for

A. shelter

B. clothing

C. play and exercise

D. moving from place to place

3SM1.2 *assess the environmental impact of structures built by various animals and those built by humans*

Structures Built by Humans and Animals

People and animals build structures for many of the same reasons. Structures can be used for shelter or to help gather food. People also build structures to help get around.

Both people and animals build structures that even use some of the same building materials. People can use wood, snow, or mud to build homes. Animals also use sticks, mud, or snow to build homes.

The Inuit people of Canada's north once built homes from snow. They cut and shaped blocks of snow. The blocks were used like bricks.

Mother polar bears dig a den in deep snow to have their young. Inside, the mother and babies stay warm and comfortable.

Animals use earth materials mostly as they find them. But people often change earth materials to build their structures. Mud can be baked into hard bricks. Rocks can be crushed and mixed with water to make concrete. People mine iron ore from the earth to make steel. The ore is melted and mixed with other things. This makes the steel very strong.

Some structures in nature have benefits for more than just the animal who builds it. Beaver dams provide food and shelter to many animals. Baby fish can hide easily in the deep water. There is a lot to eat. The quiet water lets them grow big and strong. Water birds have a calm place to build their nests. Dams also control flooding from heavy rain. Beaver dams can also help remove farm chemicals from the water.

Beaver dam

The structures people make can sometimes harm the environment. Many of the materials to build structures come from nature. People use a lot of resources to build their structures. Now, Earth is in danger of running out of some resources. Also, land needs to be cleared to make room for human structures. Plants and animals lose their homes. When people are finished with their structures, they often can not be recycled.

People have begun to realize their impact on nature. Many structures are now designed to be made with recycled materials. Some are designed to be recycled when their purpose has been served. Buildings are now being built to use less energy and water to save resources.

Use the following information to answer the next question

Keira looks at a beaver dam in a pond. She knows that the dam is good for other animals that live in the pond.

3. A beaver dam in a pond helps birds that live near the pond because it

A. helps their eggs hatch faster

B. lowers the water level in the pond

C. keeps the beavers away from their nests

D. gives the birds a calm place to build their nests

CHALLENGER QUESTION

Use the following information to answer the next question

An owl was living in Tim's backyard. It had built a nest in a hole in an old oak tree. When the owl is finished with the nest, it will move on. Other animals will use the hole in the tree for shelter.

4. Which of the following animals will **most likely** use the hole once the owl has gone?

A. 

B. 

C. 

D. 

3SM3.1 *define a structure as a supporting framework, with a definite size, shape, and purpose, that holds a load*

DESCRIBING STRUCTURES

The main goal of a structure is to support a load. Each structure is a framework that has a certain shape and size. Each structure has a certain purpose. The shape and size of a structure is guided by its purpose. What will the structure be used for? Will it carry things from place to place? Will it need to hold heavy loads? How big will it need to be?

There are many different kinds of structures. Structures are made by nature, animals, and people. Trees, nests, and hives are part of nature. Fences, buildings, and bridges are all built by people.

Some structures are meant to move a load from one place to another. A bicycle only carries one person around at a time. It does not need to be as big as a car. A car can carry many people at one time. A transport truck that carries goods from one place to another is very big.

A bridge is meant to stay in one place and let things move across the top of it. It needs to be strong and stable to hold the moving loads. There are many different shapes for bridges. Different bridge shapes are used depending on what the bridge's job will be.

A beam bridge is strong, but it can not reach very far.

Suspension bridges can cross very long distances.

An igloo and a tepee were both used as homes. But they have very different shapes. An igloo has a dome shape and is made of snow. The dome shape of the igloo is very strong. It is strong enough that a person could walk on the roof and not fall through!

A tepee has a cone shape. The cone shape is made by the poles used to make the frame. Bark or animal skins were stretched over the frame to make the walls.

Use the following information to answer the next question

A group of experts were designing a bridge. The bridge had to cross a very wide river. They decided to build a suspension bridge.

5. Which of the following reasons is the **most likely** reason that they chose to build a suspension bridge?
   - A. The bridge crosses a long distance.
   - B. It is the easiest type of bridge to build.
   - C. More traffic can cross this kind of bridge.
   - D. People will have a better view of the river.

3SM3.2 *identify structures in the natural environment and in the built environment*

Identifying Structures

Structures in Nature

Many structures are found in nature. A tree is a structure found in nature. There are parts of the tree that give it strength so it can stand up straight. The trunk of the tree gets thicker as the tree gets older. The roots of the tree hold it firmly in the ground. The roots keep the tree from falling over. The roots keep it balanced.

Some structures are made by animals. A beehive is a structure made by bees. A colony of bees finds a nice hollow space to build their home. Their bodies make beeswax. They use this wax to make many small cells. Each cell is the same size and shape. The cells line up in rows. Many cells attached together are called a honeycomb. In one part of the hive, bees use the honeycomb to store the nectar they collect. In the cells, the nectar slowly turns into honey. In another part of the hive, the queen bee lays eggs in the cells. Each cell is home to one baby bee.

The size of a beehive depends on how many bees live in it. Some beehives can be home to as many as 40 000 bees at one time.

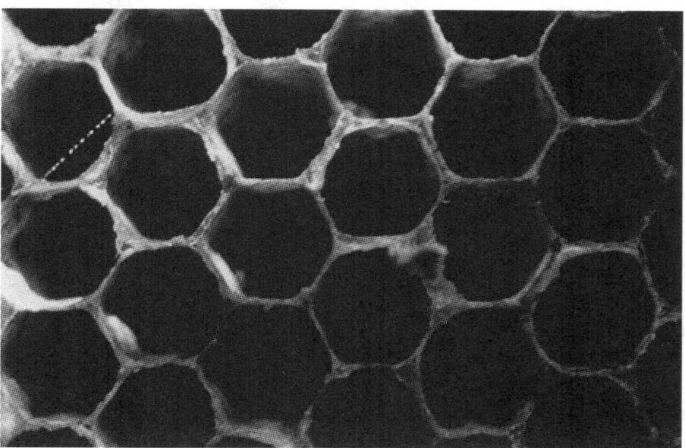

Bees use the cells in a honeycomb to store food and lay eggs.

Structures Made by People

People have been making structures for a long time. The size and shape of these structures was often affected by the materials available to them.

Some of the oldest structures on Earth are the pyramids in Egypt. They are about 4 500 years old. The pyramids are made of huge blocks of stone. Stone is very strong. The pyramids have a wide base. This makes them stable. The pyramids have lasted so long because they were well built.

The First Nations people of the West Coast make totem poles. Totem poles are tall logs carved with figures and faces. Some are of animals, and some are of people. There are many different kinds of totem poles. Some totem poles are used as supports inside a house. They are used to hold up the roof beams. Some are used on the outside of the house. They have a carved opening for people to enter the home. Some poles are decorated to remember a person who has passed away. Others are used to welcome visitors to a community.

To put up a totem pole, a deep hole is dug into the ground. Many people work together to raise the totem pole into place. They use ropes to guide it into the hole. Everyone celebrates when a totem pole is raised.

A doorway has been carved into the bottom of this pole.

Practice

6. Which of the following structures is a natural structure?

A. 

B. 

C. 

D. 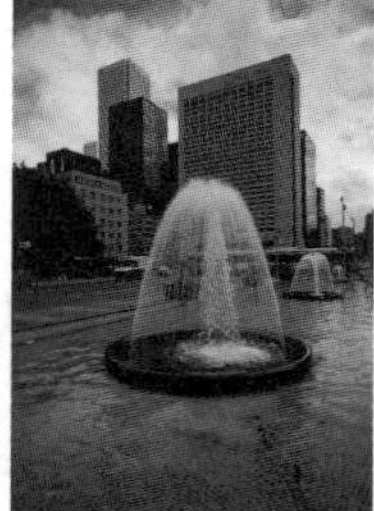

7. Which of the following structures is made by people from all natural materials?

A. Beaver lodge

B. Traditional tepee

C. Canadian Museum of Nature

D. Dragon Mountain Rollercoaster

3SM3.3 *identify the strength of a structure as its ability to support a load*

3SM3.4 *identify the stability of a structure as its ability to maintain balance and stay fixed in one spot*

Strength and Balance

Structures need to be strong so they can support a **load**. The load is the amount of weight an object can hold. Weight is the force of gravity. Gravity pulls on things and makes them heavy. **Strength** is the ability of a structure to hold up a load. A structure is strong if it can hold a lot of weight.

Sometimes, the load is the structure itself. There is no large weight on the top of a flag pole. The load is the metal of the flag pole itself.

A bridge is a man-made structure. A bridge supports very heavy loads. It must support the cement and metal it is made from. It must also support the cars and trucks that drive on it.

A bird's nest is a natural structure. The nest must be able to support the weight of the parents and the baby birds.

Structures also need to have stability. **Stability** is the ability of a structure to stay balanced and stay in one spot. Different forces push on structures. Structures need to be able to stay in place in the wind.

They need to be able to balance. This structure must stay upright even as the water washes around it.

People and animals also push on structures.

Practice

Use the following information to answer the next question

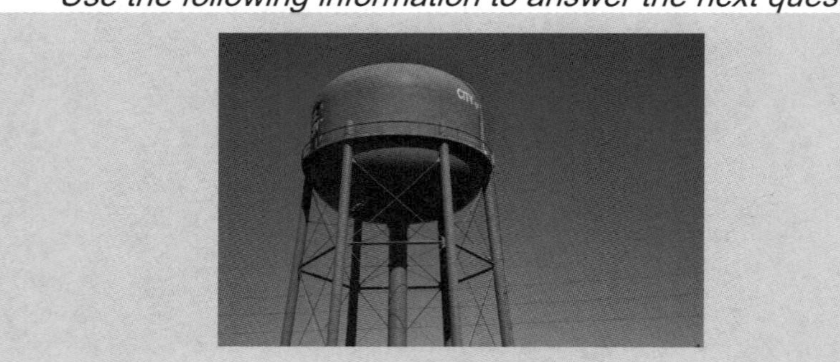

8. This water tower must be designed so that it
   - A. rusts when it gets wet
   - B. is seen from a great distance
   - C. stops taking in water when it is full
   - D. supports the weight of the water that is in it

Use the following information to answer the next question

Sasha was learning how to ski. Her instructor gave her a set of ski poles. When Sasha was going downhill, she leaned on the ski poles when she felt like she was going to fall over.

9. The **main** purpose of using ski poles when skiing is to
   - A. protect your hands if you fall over
   - B. increase your stability when skiing
   - C. keep your skis from crossing over each other
   - D. decrease the amount of strength that you need

3SM3.5 *identify properties of materials that need to be considered when building structures*

Properties of Materials

Structures need to be made out of something. The materials chosen need to be able to handle the forces acting on the structure. Strength, flexibility, and durability are three things to think about when choosing materials.

Strength

Materials need to be strong. Strength is a structure's ability to carry a load. The force of gravity is always pulling down on structures. The materials used need to be able to hold up to the force of gravity. Even when there are no cars on a bridge, gravity is still pulling down on the bridge.

The materials need to be strong enough to hold up the structure and carry a load. They have to be strong enough that they will not break, stretch, or twist. Snow on a roof adds weight. The roof must be strong enough to hold the weight of the snow.

Flexibility

Flexibility is how much a material can bend before it breaks. Some materials can hold up to forces better if they can bend. Very tall skyscrapers bend in the wind. People on the top floors can feel the building moving. It is safer if the building bends a little.

The very top of the CN Tower can move as much as 1 metre on a windy day.

Durability

Durability is how long a material can last before it wears out. Outdoor structures have to last through the heat of summer and the cold of winter. When materials get warm, they get a little bit bigger. When they get very cold, they get a little smaller. Over the year, the material is always stretching and shrinking. This can wear it out.

The force of wind and other loads put stress on materials too. These loads can cause materials to bend. It can weaken them over time.

Use the following information to answer the next question

A group of mountain climbers have set up a tent. They plan to use the tent as a base camp during the summer. They are going to climb different peaks in the area. The tent must last all summer. It must be able to hold up to bad weather.

10. When choosing the tent, they should look for one that is

A. tall **B.** strong **C.** smooth **D.** colourful

Use the following information to answer the next question

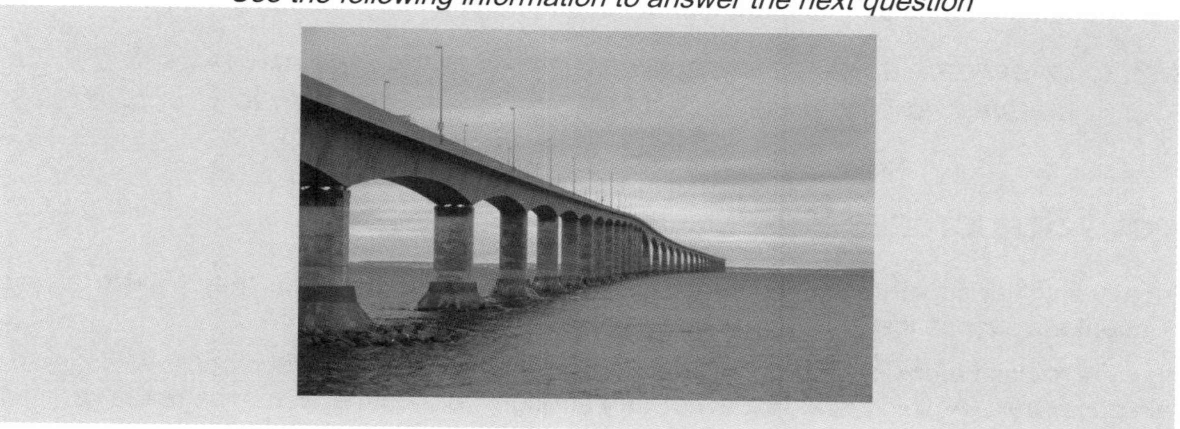

11. Bridges must be built with durable materials because the
    - **A.** colour of the materials fades after being in the sun for many days
    - **B.** colour of the materials gets brighter when acid falls falls on them
    - **C.** materials gets bigger in cold weather and smaller in cold weather
    - **D.** materials gets smaller in cold weather and bigger in warm weather

3SM3.6 *describe ways in which the strength of different materials can be altered*

3SM2.2 *investigate, through experimentation, how various materials and construction techniques can be used to add strength to structures*

Making Structures Stronger

Builders want their structures to be strong. They think about the materials they will use. They think about the shapes they will form with those materials.

If you were to build a box, you could choose to use paper or wood. A wood box is stronger than a plain paper box. A plain paper box is not very strong at all. But paper can be made stronger. Cardboard is made of paper. The paper has been folded and layered. Folding and layering the paper makes the cardboard stronger. The extra paper helps to make the cardboard stronger. The shape of the folded layer also makes the cardboard stronger. Stronger cardboard will make a stronger box.

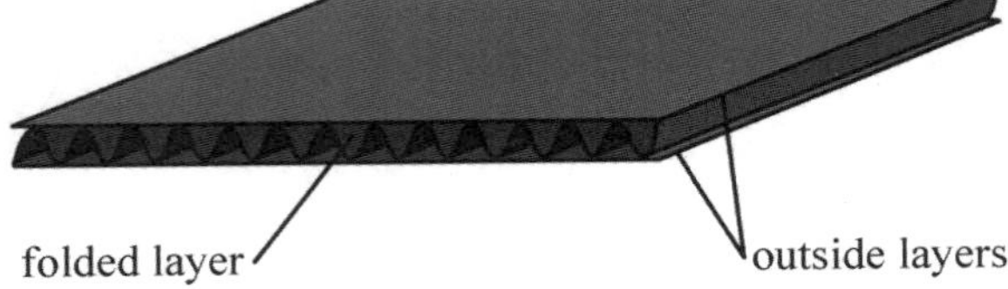

The fold inside the cardboard makes it stronger.

String is also used to build structures. Look closely at a piece of string. String is made of many different threads. The threads are twisted together. Twisting and braiding makes string stronger. Wire cables are twisted and braided to make them stronger too.

Wire cables are twisted together for strength.

Another way to make things stronger is to change their shape. Triangles are a strong shape. You can see the triangle shape used in bridges and other structures.

This bridge is stronger because of the triangular shapes used.

An arch is another strong shape. Many structures have used arches. Some arches are so strong they have been standing for over 1 500 years.

The Roman aqueducts carried water to cities from faraway places. Many cities still use them today.

Practice

Use the following information to answer the next question

Nathan is making a bridge out of two thin pieces of cardboard, paper drinking cups, and glue. He needs the bridge to be strong and stable.

12. Which picture shows the **best** way that Nathan can use the cardboard and paper cups to make a strong bridge?

A. 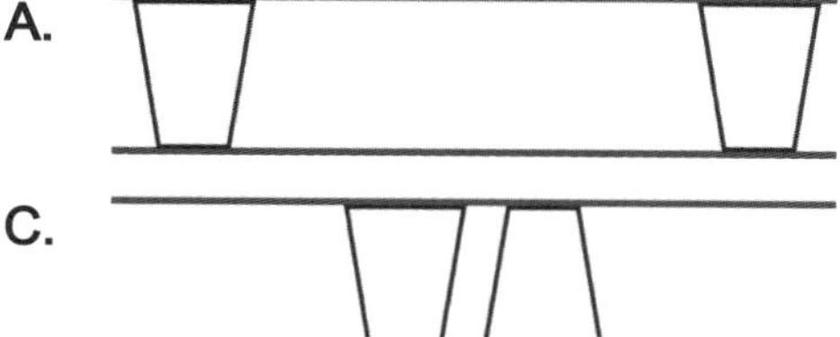

B. 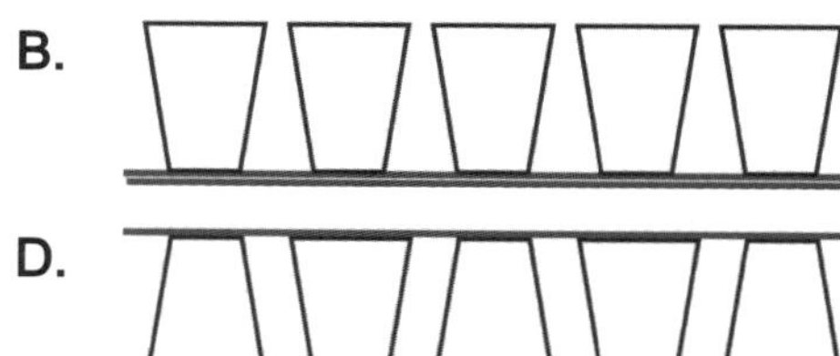

C.

D.

Use the following information to answer the next question

These wire cables are twisted and braided together.

13. Wire cables are twisted or braided together to make

A. a structure lighter

B. the wire cables stronger

C. the wire cables easier to handle

D. it easier to wrap new wires around these braids

Use the following information to answer the next question

Josie wants to use a cardboard box to move some heavy school books to her new house.

14. To increase the strength of the bottom of the cardboard box, she should

A. line the bottom of the box with tissue paper

B. tape the top of the box closed when it is full

C. crumple some newspaper at the bottom of the box

D. add more layers of cardboard to the bottom of the box

3SM3.7 *describe ways to improve a structure's strength and stability*

3SM2.3 *investigate, through experimentation, the effects of pushing, pulling, and other forces on the shape and stability of simple structures*

3SM3.10 *identify the role of struts and ties in structures under load*

Ways to Increase Strength

Some shapes are stronger than others. Triangles are strong shapes. If you push down on the top of a triangle, it does not change shape easily. A square or rectangle shape is not as sturdy. If you push down on them, they will change shape more easily. You can add strength to your structure by making or adding triangular shapes.

You can see triangles in many kinds of structures.

Struts and ties can add strength to a structure.

A **strut** is a brace used to act against compression. **Compression** is the force that pushes on structures. The weight of a load causes compression. A strut resists this pushing force by pushing back. This gives support. Struts are often the upright pieces in a structure. They are usually made of strong materials such as wood or metal bars.

A **tie** is used to act against tension. **Tension** is the pulling force that stretches materials apart. The weight of a load can put tension on a structure. A tie resists this pulling force by not allowing the structure to spread apart. This gives support.

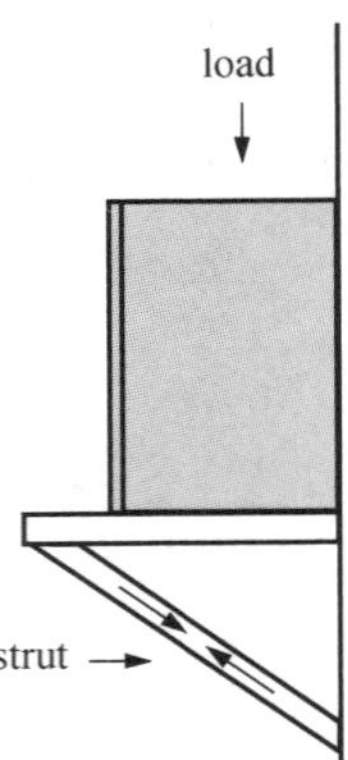

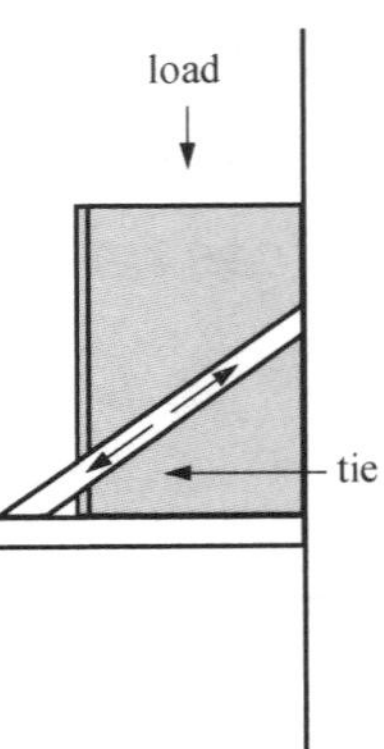

The weight of the book and the shelf is pushing down on the strut. The strut acts against the force of compression.

The weight of the book and the shelf is pulling down on the tie. The tie acts against the force of tension.

Many homes are built using struts and ties. The roof of your house may use struts and ties to hold the weight of the roof. In Canada, roofs also need to hold up the weight of snow in wintertime.

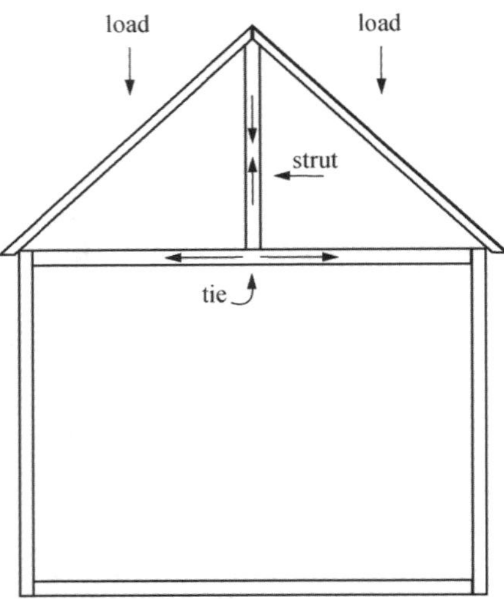

The weight of the roof pushes down on the strut. The tie stops the sides from pulling apart.

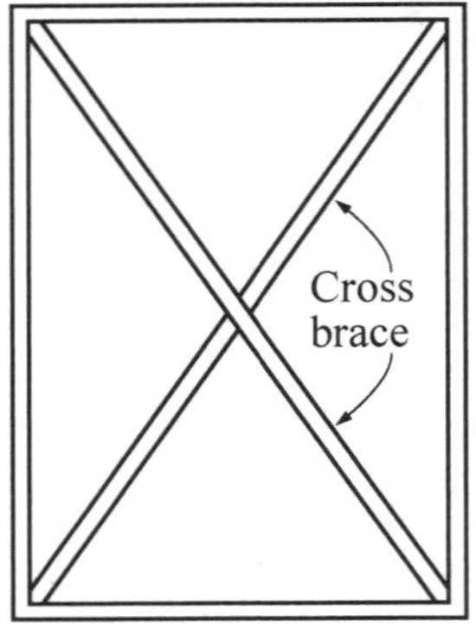

Cross braces are another way to make structures sturdier. Cross braces are two pieces that form an X shape. They are made with strong materials. They attach to a square or rectangle shape in the structure. Cross braces help a structure hold up to compression and tension.

Ways to Increase Stability

Structures need to be stable. They need to be able to balance and stay in one spot. Wind and other forces can push on structures.

A structure's centre of gravity helps it balance. It is the place on a structure where the weight is balanced in all directions. Builders think about where to put weight on their structures. A structure with too much weight at the top could be pushed over easily. A structure is more stable if the centre of gravity is lower. Builders will add weight to the bottom of a structure to make it more stable.

Putting more weight at the bottom of a structure makes it more stable.

Changing a structure's shape can also change its centre of gravity. Stand with your feet together, and ask a friend to try to push you off balance. Then stand with your feet wide apart and try again. You should find it easier to keep your balance the second time. Structures that are wider at the bottom than the top are more stable.

Practice

Use the following information to answer the next question

Odelia's mother wants a new worktable. She wants to use it to repot her house plants. The table needs to be strong. It needs to hold heavy bags of soil.

15. Which of the following tables is the strongest?

A.
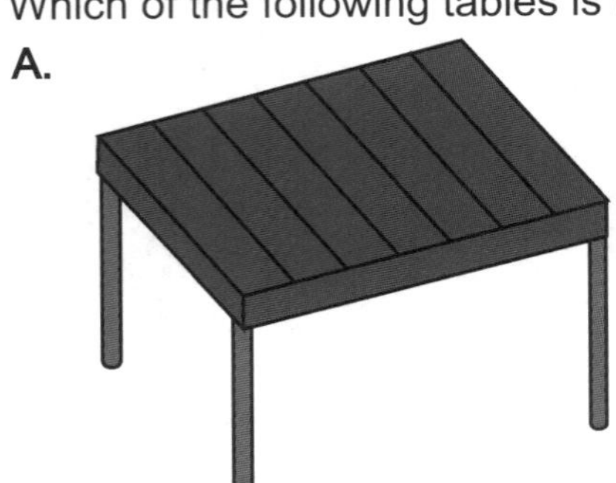

B.

C.

D.

16. Which of the following shapes is the strongest?

A. Square
B. Octagon
C. Triangle
D. Rectangle

Use the following information to answer the next question

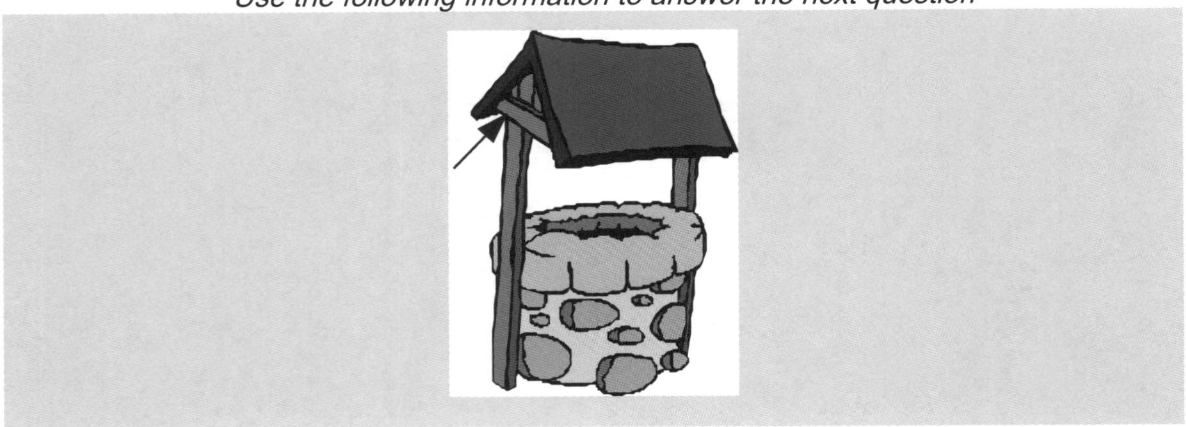

17. The wooden beam the arrow is pointing to is called a

A. tie
B. link
C. load
D. strut

Use the following information to answer the next question

Theodore wants to use a wheelbarrow to move some bricks. He is worried that his wheelbarrow will not hold a lot of weight. Theodore wants to find a way to support the bricks better. He decides to add some pieces of wood to the bottom of the wheelbarrow.

18. Which of the following diagrams shows the **best** way to add support to the wheelbarrow?

A. 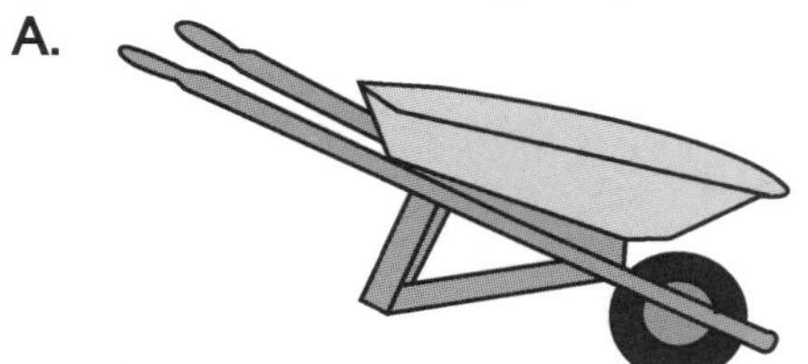

B. 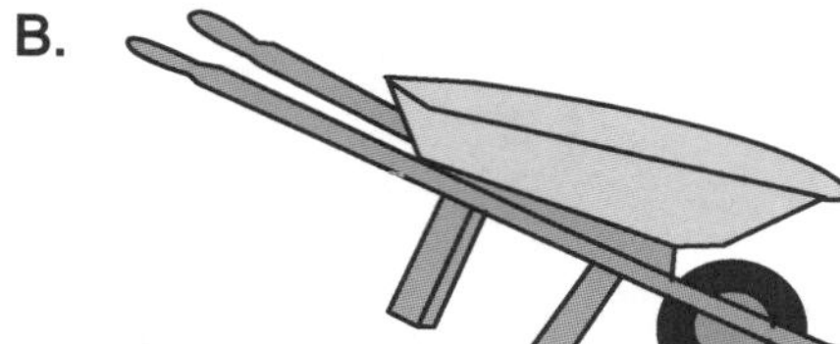

C. 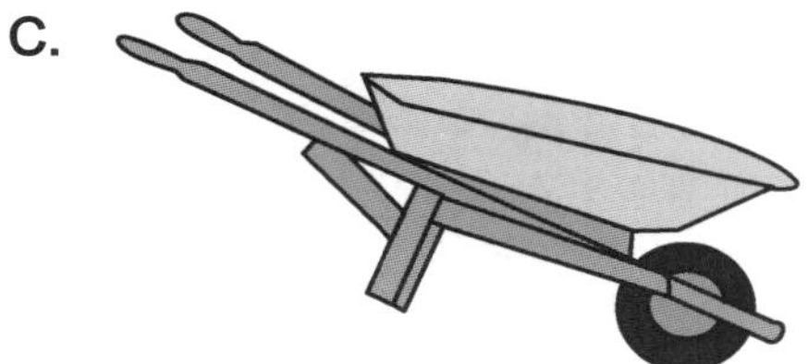

D. 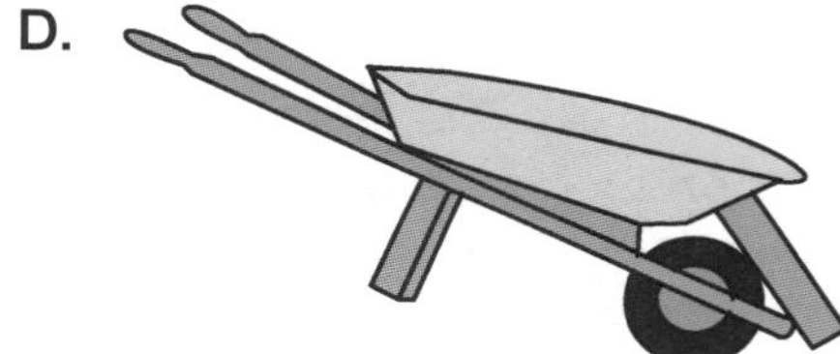

3SM3.8 *explain how strength and stability enable a structure to perform a specific function*

How Strength and Stability Affect the Purpose of Structures

Different structures are used for different things. What a structure will be used for affects how it will be built. Structures that carry a heavy load need to be built much stronger than structures that do not.

Bridges need to be strong and stable. A bridge needs to be able to hold up the weight of cars, trucks, and people. Big transport trucks carry heavy loads. There may be more than one on a bridge at a time. A bridge also has to be able to stand up to the weather. Wind and extreme temperatures can put a lot of force on a bridge. A bridge also has to last a long time.

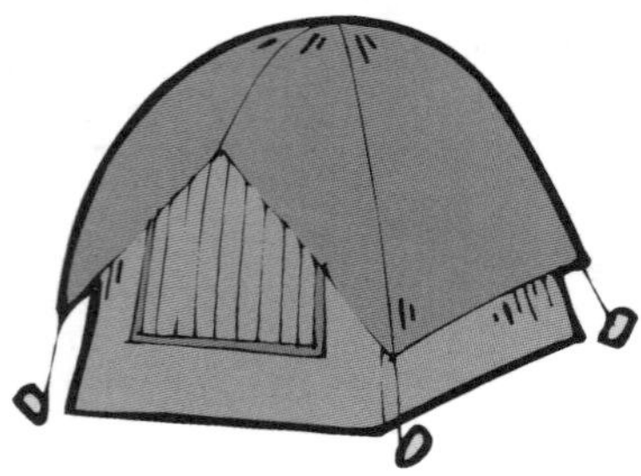

The materials used for a tent do not have to be as sturdy as they do for a bridge. A tent does not have to carry a heavy load. The tent poles only have to carry the weight of the tent fabric. A tent also has to be light enough for a person to carry. A tent is a temporary shelter. It does not have to stay up for a long time. It can be set up and taken down quickly and easily. The poles need to be able to fold up or come apart.

**Practice**

19. Which of the following structures must be made with materials that can handle very heavy loads?

A. 

B. 

C. 

D. 

Use the following information to answer the next question

Edessa is looking at pictures of houses from around the world. She notices that some of the houses have a flat roof. Some houses have a very steep roof with a high peak.

20. Which of the following houses does **not** have the best roof for holding up a load of snow?

A.

B.

C.

D.

3SM3.9 *describe ways in which different forces can affect the shape, balance, or position of structures*

How Forces Affect Structures

Forces can change the shape, balance, or position of structures. Structures need to be strong and stable enough to hold up to these forces.

If the load is too heavy for a structure, it can bend. If it bends too much, the structure can break. A cardboard box is strong. It can hold a heavy load. However, if the load is too heavy, the sides can buckle. This weakens the cardboard. It is not as strong as it was before.

The materials in a structure can change shape if they are stretched or twisted. If they stretch or twist too much, they can also break. An elastic band can stretch far. If you stretch it too far, it will break.

Forces can make a structure fall over or move. Strong wind blowing on a structure can make it fall over. A wide base helps a structure hold up to the force of wind.

A structure like a building or a bridge needs to be held in place. Vibrations from loads moving across can make a bridge change positions over time. A bridge needs to be anchored into the ground in some way. Many tall buildings have supports that go many stories into the ground. This helps the building stand tall.

This bridge is attached to the ground by the poles on the river bank.

Practice

Use the following information to answer the next question

This type of rope bridge is often found in the wilderness. They often cross rivers or large gaps. Rope bridges are strong enough for people to walk across. However, they bend and swing under the weight.

21. The structure of a rope bridge will change the **most** when there is more

A. rain **B.** wind **C.** weight **D.** sunshine

Use the following information to answer the next question

Many different objects are made with materials that are designed to bend a certain amount without breaking.

22. Which of the following objects will bend the **least** before breaking?

A. Metal golf club
B. Soft rubber tubing
C. Glass window pane
D. Wooden hockey stick

3SM2.1 *follow established safety procedures during science and technology investigations*

Safety Rules

During this unit, you may be building your own stable structures. Here are some safety rules to remember:

- Always follow instructions carefully. If you need help, ask your teacher or an adult.
- Keep your workspace tidy. This will prevent accidents.
- Always carry cutting tools, such as scissors, with the sharp end pointed away from yourself and others. Walk. Do not run.
- Clean up after yourself. Make sure all materials are put back where they belong.

Practice

23. Which of the following tables correctly matches building materials and tools with safe storage places?

A.

Tool/Material	Storage Place
Hammer	Workbench
Saw	Shelf
Nails	Toolbox
Glue	Pegboard

B.

Tool/Material	Storage Place
Hammer	Pegboard
Saw	Toolbox
Nails	Floor
Glue	Toolbox

C.

Tool/Material	Storage Place
Hammer	Toolbox
Saw	Pegboard
Nails	Toolbox
Glue	Shelf

D.

Tool/Material	Storage Place
Hammer	Floor
Saw	Workbench
Nails	Shelf
Glue	Toolbox

Use the following information to answer the next question

Fergal borrowed a pair of scissors to build his paper tower. He was asked to bring the scissors he was using to the front table.

24. What is the **safest** way for Fergal to carry the scissors to the front table?

A. Run and hold the blades inward facing his body

B. Walk and hold the blades inward facing his body

C. Run and hold the blades outward away from his body

D. Walk and hold the blades outward away from his body

3SM2.4 *use technological problem-solving skills, and knowledge acquired from previous investigations, to design and build a strong and stable structure that serves a purpose*

Building Strong and Stable Structures

At some point in this unit, you will be asked to build a structure. Keep these things in mind as you build:

- What is the purpose of your structure?
- What forces will affect this structure?
- What materials will you use?
- How will you make the structure strong?
- How will you make the structure stable?

Here is an example. Charlie's classroom gets cluttered. His teacher asks him to build a structure for the students' lunch bags. The purpose is to store all the lunches. Some of the lunches are heavy. There is not a lot of room on the table. He decides to make shelves. The shelves will need to be strong and stable.

Charlie thinks about what to use to make the shelves. Cardboard and paper are too weak. Wood and metal are strong. Charlie decides to build the shelves out of wood.

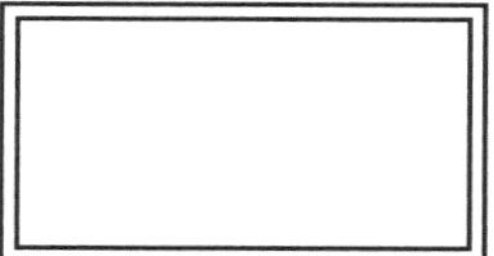

Charlie thinks about the form or shape of the structure. Charlie looks around the classroom. He notices that the shelves in the classroom are all rectangle shapes. He decides to use a rectangular shape.

Charlie builds the rectangular shape with the help of his older brother. The walls are strong but are not stable. The walls wobble from side to side.

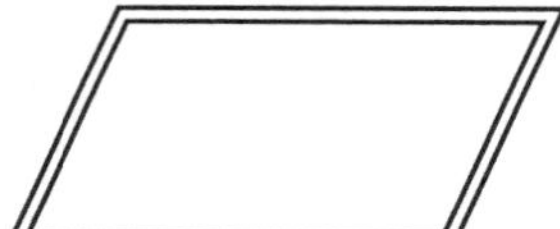

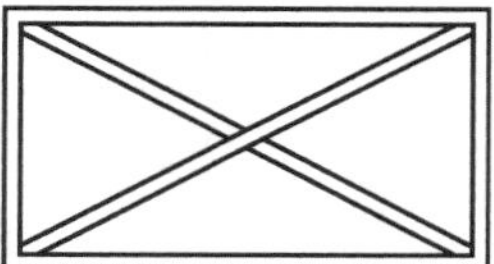

Charlie knows that triangles are stable. He puts 2 struts across the back of the rectangle. Now, there are 4 triangles.

The struts make the rectangle stable. Charlie adds the shelves. Now, there is a strong, stable place for the lunches.

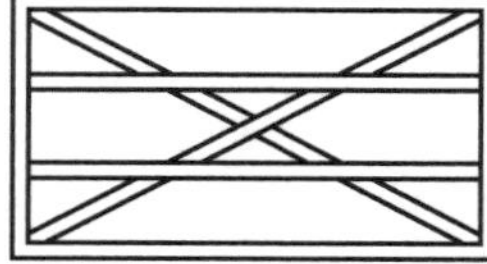

Practice

Use the following information to answer the next question

Tiffany is planning to build a stable brick wall. She draws a design on a piece of paper before she begins her project.

25. Which of the following designs is the **most** stable?

A. 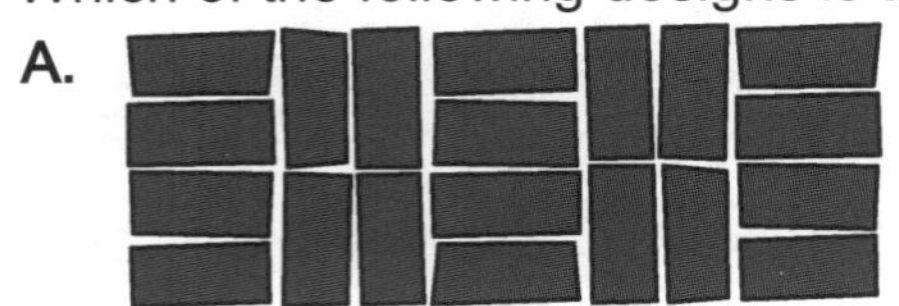

B. 

C.

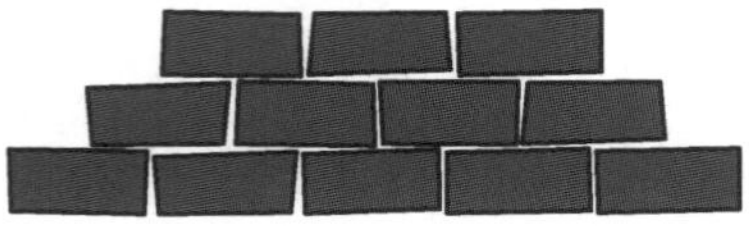

D.

Use the following information to answer the next question

Sam helped her father build a wooden compost bin. They are going to add dirt, grass clippings, and vegetable scraps. Eventually, the bin will get very full.

26. Sam and her father chose this design for the compost bin because the

A. sides are short

B. wood will not rot over time

C. dirt can not be piled too high

D. cross braces make the bin more stable

3SM2.5 *use appropriate science and technology vocabulary, including compression, tension, strut, ties, strength, and stability, in oral and written communication*

Vocabulary

Please look in the glossary to find the following vocabulary words: **compression**, **tension**, **strut**, **ties**, **strength**, and **stability**.

27. What is a tie used for in a structure?
    - A. It stops weight from pushing down on the structure.
    - B. It prevents the structure from cracking.
    - C. It acts against the force of compression.
    - D. It acts against the force of tension.

SOLUTIONS—STRUCTURES AND MECHANISMS: STRONG AND STABLE STRUCTURES

1. B	7. B	13. B	19. B	25. C
2. A	8. D	14. D	20. D	26. D
3. D	9. B	15. D	21. C	27. D
4. C	10. B	16. C	22. C	
5. A	11. C	17. A	23. C	
6. A	12. D	18. A	24. D	

1. B

The fence made of brick will most likely last the longest. Brick is a strong building material. It will last longer than wood.

2. A

Both people and animals use structures for shelter. Gathering and storing food is another use of structures shared by people and animals.

3. D

A beaver dam forms a pond where it blocks a stream. This gives waterbirds a calm and quiet place to build their nests.

4. C

The most likely animal to use the tree for shelter is the woodpecker. Woodpeckers build nests in tree holes. They eat the bugs that live underneath the bark.

5. A

A suspension bridge is often built across a wide river or body of water. They are used because they can cross a long distance.

6. A

Waterfalls are a natural structure. Some waterfalls formed when the glaciers receded at the end of the last ice age.

7. B

Traditional tepees were made using all natural materials. People made them by using three long poles and an animal skin or birch bark. The three poles were tied together and then stood upright. The animal skin or bark was then stretched around the three poles to form a shelter.

8. D

The water tower must be designed so that it can support the weight of the water that is in it. It must also be able to support the material that the water tower is made out of.

9. B

Using ski poles when you are skiing helps you balance. The main purpose of using ski poles is to increase your stability when skiing.

10. B

When choosing the tent, the climbers should look for a tent that is made of a strong material. A strong material will be better able to withstand any severe weather that may occur.

11. C

The materials used to construct a bridge must be durable. The materials will get a little bigger in warm weather and a little smaller in cold weather. These materials must be able to change year after year without breaking.

12. D

The platform with all the paper cups in between the two layers of cardboard would make the strongest bridge. The paper cups provide more support evenly throughout the structure.

13. B

Twisting and braiding wire cables makes them stronger. Just like string, wire cables can be twisted together and braided for this purpose.

14. D

Extra layers at the bottom of the box will make it stronger. Folding and layering makes cardboard stronger.

15. D

The worktable with cross braces is the strongest structure. This table would best hold up the plants and heavy bags of soil.

16. C

Triangular shapes are used in buildings and structures because a triangle shape is the strongest.

17. A

The support beam that stops the sides of the roof from pulling apart is called a tie.

18. A

By adding a cross brace on the bottom, it makes a triangle-shaped support. This shape is strong and adds support to the wheelbarrow. The wheelbarrow will then be able to carry a heavy load.

19. B

A bridge must be strong enough to stand upright. It also must withstand the load of the traffic that crosses it. Bridges must be built with materials that are strong enough to handle these loads.

20. D

A house with a flat roof is not the best roof for holding up a load of snow. Peaked roofs form a triangle. Snow is heavy. A triangle is a strong shape for heavy loads.

21. C

A rope bridge is designed to bend and stretch under the weight of the people crossing it. If there is too much weight on the bridge, it will most likely break. More rain, wind, or sunshine will not change the structure of a rope bridge.

22. C

Glass will not bend. If you try to bend glass, it will break. Soft rubber tubing is made to be bendable. The golf club and hockey stick will bend a little, but they too will break with a lot of pressure.

23. C

It is important to store and put materials back where they belong. Hammers and nails belong in a toolbox, and a saw belongs on a pegboard. Glue belongs on a shelf.

24. D

The safest way to carry sharp tools is to face the blades outward away from your body. Never run with sharp tools. Always walk. When running, there is more chance of tripping and falling than walking.

25. C

The design with the bricks that overlap each other is the most stable structure.

26. D

The cross braces make the compost bin stronger and more stable.

27. D

A tie is a support. It is used to act against the force of tension.

NOTES

Unit Test

1. Which of the following structures is **least likely** to be recycled by nature?

A.

B.

C.

D.

Use the following information to answer the next question

A shopping mall is to be built just outside the city limits. To build the mall, all of the trees in a forest must be cut down.

2. A harmful effect of building the shopping mall is that
   A. the animals in the forest will lose their homes
   B. many people will do their shopping at the mall
   C. building the mall will increase the number of jobs in the area
   D. clearing the land will make more room for houses to be built nearby

3. Which of the following structures is made from materials that can be recycled by nature?

A.

B.

C.

D.

Use the following information to answer the next question

Randy was going on a hiking trip. He planned to hike a long distance over many different types of trails. Randy wanted a pair of shoes that cushioned his heels and supported his feet.

4. Which of the following pairs of shoes is **best** for hiking?

A. 

B. 

C. 

D. 

Use the following information to answer the next question

Emily was studying structures. She made a chart of structures that were built by nature and those that were made by people.

Emily noticed that she had made a mistake in her chart.

Nature	**People**
Beehive	Radio tower
Tepee	Fence
Bird's nest	Flag pole

5. Which of the following structures is **not** in the correct column?

A. Tent
B. Tepee
C. Flag pole
D. Radio tower

6. Which of the following chairs would **most likely** break under a heavy weight?

A. 

B. 

C. 

D. 

Use the following information to answer the next question

Paul was riding a bicycle. He stopped at a stop sign to let the cars go by. He slowed his bike down until he was hardly moving.

7. What should Paul do so that he will not fall over when he comes to a stop?
   - A. Change gears.
   - B. Put his feet on the ground.
   - C. Turn his wheels to the side.
   - D. Hold the handlebars tightly.

Use the following information to answer the next question

Trevor looks at pictures of different types of structures.

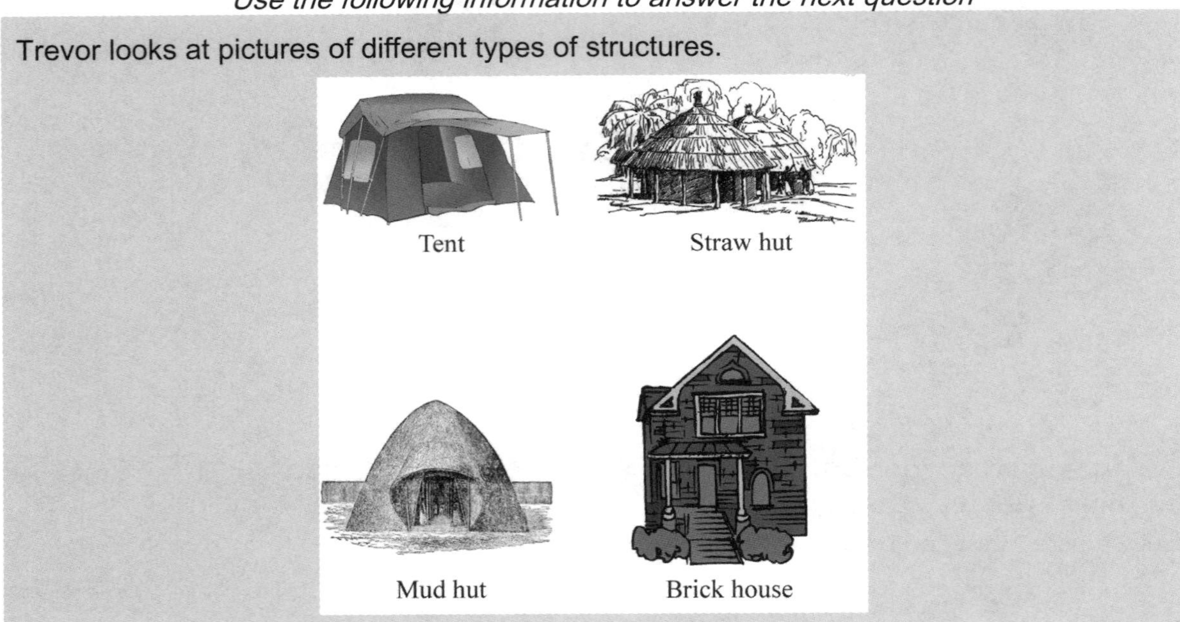

8. The structure built with the strongest material is the
   - A. tent
   - B. mud hut
   - C. straw hut
   - D. brick house

Use the following information to answer the next question

Hayley is getting ready to fly her kite on a windy day. She has four long, thin strings to choose from to attach to her kite. Hayley knows that each of the strings are not going to be strong enough against the high winds.

9. To make the strings stronger, Hayley could
   - A. tie each string to the kite separately
   - B. only use two of the strongest looking strings
   - C. braid the four strings together to make one string
   - D. tie the strings end to end to make one long string

Use the following information to answer the next question

1

2

3

4

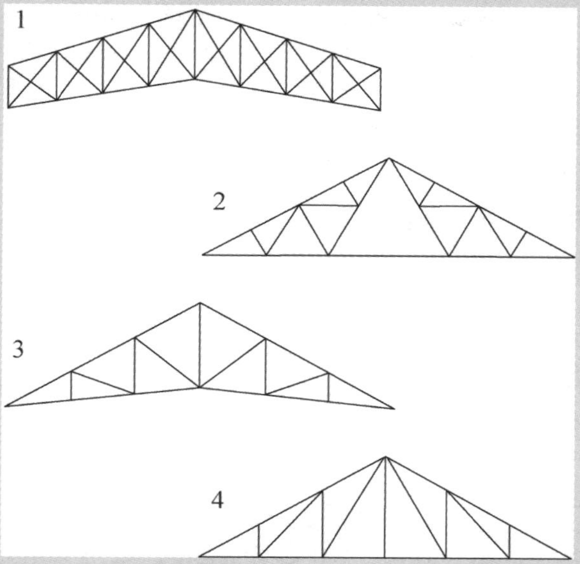

10. Which of the trusses shown **most likely** provides the greatest support for a very heavy roof?

A. 1 **B.** 2 **C.** 3 **D.** 4

Use the following information to answer the next question

Trista sees a tall pole holding up a sign. It has cables attached to it from the top of the pole to the ground. She knows that these cables help to make the pole more stable.

11. Which of the following structures also uses ropes or wires to make it more stable?

A. Chimney on a house

B. Gate in a fence

C. Bird feeder

D. Tent

Use the following information to answer the next question

Camryn and Dan were testing the strength of a small cardboard box. They began by placing the empty cardboard box on the floor. Camryn collected a number of bricks that were the same size as the cardboard box. Dan began stacking the bricks on top of the cardboard box one at a time.

12. What **most likely** happened to the cardboard box as more bricks were added on top?

A. The box slid and moved into a new position.

B. The top of the box bent outward.

C. The sides of the box buckled.

D. The box stretched inward.

Use the following information to answer the next question

Tall buildings must hold up the loads placed on them. They must also hold up to the force of the wind. Tall buildings are made with materials that bend slightly with the wind.

13. What is another way buildings are built to hold up to the wind?

A. They are made of recycled materials.

B. They have supports that go deep into the ground.

C. Tall buildings are only made with flexible materials.

D. Tall buildings have wires that anchor them to the ground.

Use the following information to answer the next question

Nina looked at the bookshelf in her room. She sees that there is a strut underneath between the shelf and the wall.

14. What is the **main** purpose of the strut underneath the bookshelf?

A. The strut acts against the tension forces of the books.

B. The strut stops the weight of the books from pushing up.

C. The strut stops the sides from pulling away from the shelf.

D. The strut acts against the compression forces of the books.

Use the following information to answer the next question

Jennifer saw this sign in her classroom at school.

15. What safety rule does this sign show?
    A. Hold scissors in one hand only.
    B. Always walk with scissors, and hold the pointed end down.
    C. Never take your eyes off the scissors when you are running.
    D. Carry scissors so that they are pointed in the air away from your body.

Use the following information to answer the next question

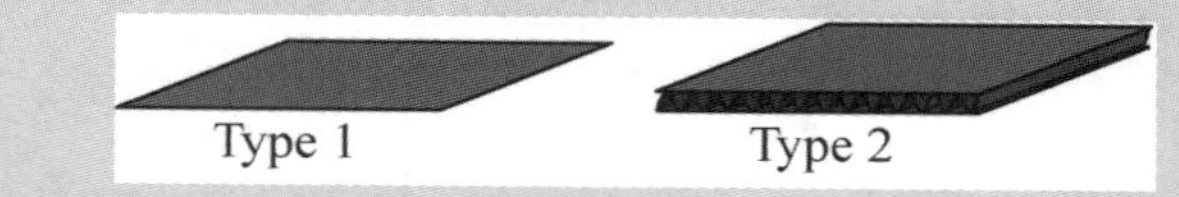

Jillian has to choose between two different types of cardboard as shown. Each type will be used to make a box to carry some items.

16. Type 2 cardboard should be stronger because the paper used to make it has been
    A. folded and layered
    B. soaked in water first
    C. bent and crumpled out of shape
    D. treated with chemicals that form its shape

Use the following information to answer the next question

Gerald built this frame out of small wooden sticks and glue. He wants to make the frame stronger by adding more wooden sticks.

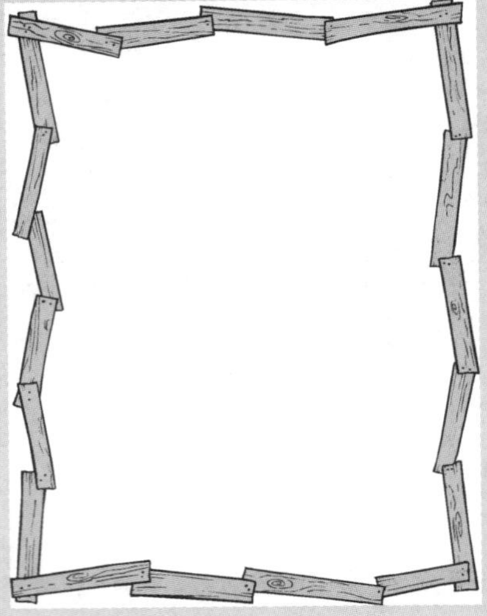

17. Which diagram shows the **strongest** frame?

A.

B.
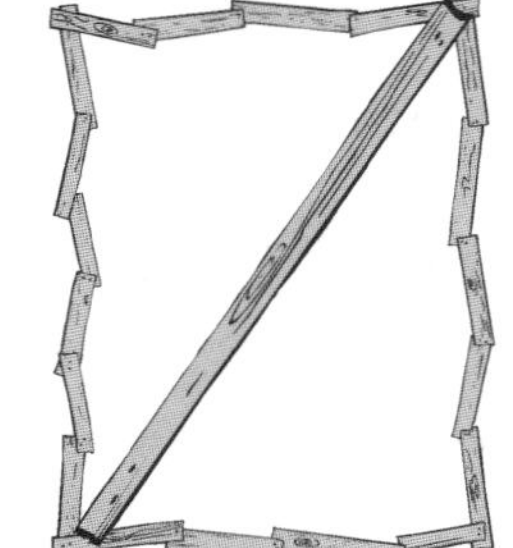

C.
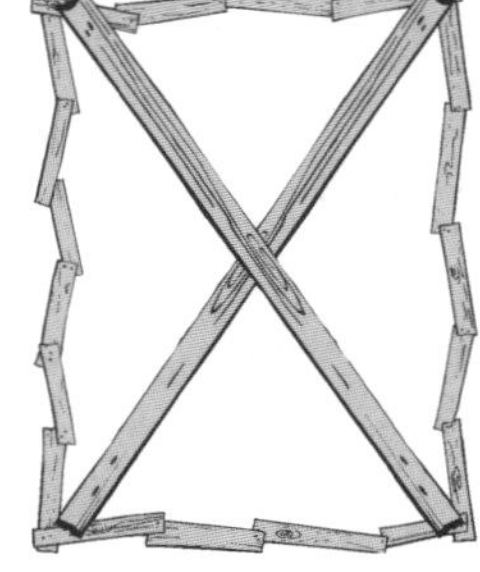

D.
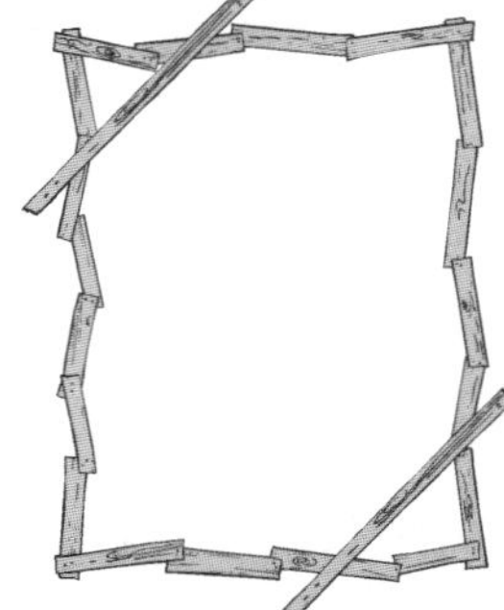

Use the following information to answer the next question

Toby built a wooden gate. He made a cross brace and attached it to the gate.

18. What is the **most likely** reason Toby added a cross brace to the gate?

A. It made the gate look better.

B. It made the gate more stable.

C. He had an extra piece of wood left over.

D. He wanted the gate to be easier to open and close.

Use the following information to answer the next question

Scott has built a newspaper tower that is 3.5 metres tall. Unfortunately, the tower keeps falling over.

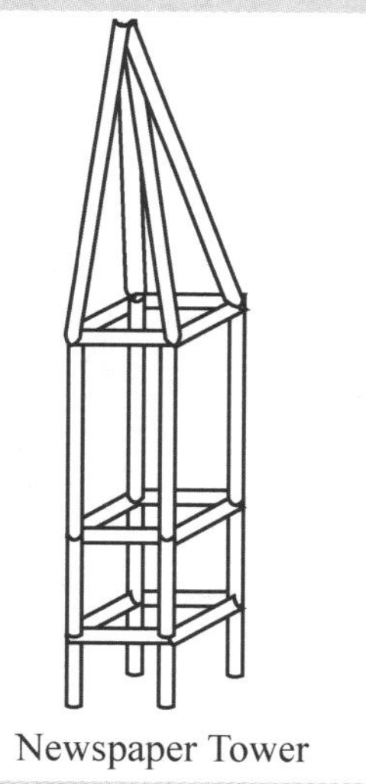

Newspaper Tower

19. To keep the tower from falling over, Scott should

A. widen the base of the tower

B. make the top of the tower wider

C. make the base of the tower smaller

D. add more weight to the top of the tower

20. The definition of tension is

A. the force that stretches things apart

B. the amount a structure is pushed together
the force that causes a structure to buckle

C. the amount of weight a structure can support

SOLUTIONS

1. D	5. B	9. C	13. B	17. C
2. A	6. D	10. A	14. D	18. B
3. D	7. B	11. D	15. B	19. A
4. C	8. D	12. C	16. A	20. A

1. D

An apartment building is least likely to be recycled by nature. Some of the materials will be recycled, but some will have to be taken to a landfill. The totem pole, spider web, and inukshuk are all made of materials that can be recycled by nature.

2. A

A harmful effect of building a shopping mall is that the animals will lose their homes. In order to build the shopping mall, all of the trees must be cut down. Many animals use the trees in the forest as their shelter.

3. D

A tepee is a traditional home built by the First Nations people. Tepees are made with logs and skins, which can be recycled by nature.

4. C

For hiking, a shoe that has a lot of support is best. The shoe will also need to have cushioning in the heel. It absorbs the force of the body pushing down as you hike.

5. B

A tepee is not built by nature. A tepee is built by people.

6. D

The folding chair is not as strong as the other types of chairs. A folding chair would most likely break under a heavy weight.

7. B

Paul should put his feet on the ground. This wil make the base of the bicycle wider. A wider base will keep the bicycle balanced and stable while he is stopped.

8. D

The brick house is built with the strongest material. It can withstand harsh weather better compared to the other houses.

9. C

The strings can be made stronger by braiding them together. One thick string will be stronger than using each string individually.

10. A

The truss with the most triangular shapes will provide the greatest support. Truss 1 has the most triangles and will most likely provide the greatest support for a very heavy roof.

11. D

A tent uses ropes to provide support. A tent is made of lightweight fabric. The ropes are all that is needed to keep the tent anchored to the ground.

12. C

The sides of the cardboard box most likely buckled under the weight of the bricks. The sides of a structure can buckle, or bend, when a heavy load is placed on top of it.

13. B

Tall buildings have supports that go deep into the ground. This helps the buildings stay upright under the force of the wind.

14. D

The bookshelf pushes down on the strut. Compression is the force that pushes down on a structure. Therefore, the strut resists the compression forces of the books.

15. B

The sign shows that when carrying scissors, it is important to hold the pointed end down and away from your body. You must also walk and not run.

16. A

The Type 2 cardboard has been folded and layered. This increases the strength of the paper that was used to make it.

17. C

Adding or joining parts of a structure to form triangles makes it much stronger. The frame shown in alternative is the strongest.

18. B

The cross brace forms a triangular shape between the bottom of the gate and the top. This triangular shape makes the gate more stable.

19. A

A tower built with a larger base will be more stable.

20. A

Tension is the force that stretches things apart.

NOTES

Forces Causing Movement

Matter and Energy: Forces Causing Movement

Table of Correlations

	Specific Expectation	Practice Questions	Unit Test Questions
3ME1:STSE	Assess the impact of various forces on society and the environment;		
3ME1.1	*assess the effects of the action of forces in nature on the natural and built environment, and identify ways in which human activities can reduce or enhance this impact*	1, 2	1, 2
3ME1.2	*assess the impact of safety devices that minimize the effects of forces in various human activities*	3, 4	3
3ME3:Concepts	Demonstrate an understanding of how forces cause movement and changes in movement.		
3ME3.1	*identify a force as a push or a pull that causes an object to move*	5	4
3ME3.2	*identify different kinds of forces*	6	5
3ME3.3	*describe how different forces applied to an object at rest can cause the object to start, stop, attract, repel, or change direction*	7	6
3ME3.4	*explain how forces are exerted through direct contact or through interaction at a distance*	8	7
3ME3.5	*identify ways in which forces are used in their daily lives*	11, 12	8
3ME2:Skills	Investigate devices that use forces to create controlled movement;		
3ME2.1	*follow established safety procedures during science and technology investigations*	13	9
3ME2.2	*investigate forces that cause an object to start moving, stop moving, or change direction*	9, 10	10, 11
3ME2.3	*conduct investigations to determine the effects of increasing or decreasing the amount of force applied to an object*	14, 15	12, 13
3ME2.4	*use technological problem-solving skills, and knowledge acquired from previous investigations, to design and build devices that use forces to create controlled movement*	16, 17	14
3ME2.5	*use appropriate science and technology vocabulary, including push, pull, load, distance, and speed, in oral and written communication*	18	15

3ME1.1 *assess the effects of the action of forces in nature on the natural and built environment, and identify ways in which human activities can reduce or enhance this impact*

Effects of Actions in Nature

Rain, wind, floods, and earthquakes are all actions caused by forces in nature. Forces in nature act on both natural and man-made structures. There is not much people can do about these forces. However, you can do things to lessen their effect.

Look at this example. Rain washes away soil. This is called erosion. If too much soil is washed away, it can pollute rivers, lakes, and streams. This is a natural process, and nature has ways to protect the soil from erosion. The roots of trees, grass, and other plants hold soil in place. When it rains, the soil does not wash away. The roots reduce the effect of erosion.

People can speed up erosion that is already happening. They can also start erosion in places where there has been little of it before. Here are some ways that people cause erosion:

- People remove trees, plants, and shrubs to clear land for farms or houses. Trees are also cut down to make paper. When the trees and plants are gone, there is nothing to hold the soil in place. It is easier for water to wash the soil away. Wind can also blow the soil away. When people cut down forests or remove plants, they remove nature's protection.
- People can put too many animals on farmland. The animals eat all the plants. Sometimes, they eat so many of the plants that the plants die. Without the plants, the soil is not held in place. It can be washed or blown away.

When a farm loses its soil, the farmer may not be able to grow plants as well. There may be so little soil left that nothing will grow well.

People have also been able to lessen erosion. Here are some ways that people have helped slow down erosion:

- People plant trees and other plants in areas where they have been removed. This helps to protect the soil.
- In some places, the way of cutting down trees for paper has changed. Instead of removing all the trees from an area, loggers only remove some of the trees.
- People can put in windbreaks to lessen the force of the wind. Farmers sometimes plant rows of trees between their fields. This prevents the soil in their fields from blowing away.

Use the following information to answer the next question

A farmer plowed his fields. He was getting ready to plant. A rainstorm came and washed the soil from the field into a nearby lake. Later, the farmer found that the fish in the lake were dying.

1. The fish in the lake died because
   - **A.** the fish in the lake were weak
   - **B.** the fish were fighting each other
   - **C.** water from the farmer's field was killing the fish
   - **D.** soil from the farmer's field was polluting the lake

Use the following information to answer the next question

A steep hillside was cleared so that new houses could be built on it. All of the trees and plants were removed to make it easier to build houses. The houses were built near the top of the hill. A sudden, heavy rainfall fell in the area. A landslide of mud happened that damaged some of the houses.

2. To prevent the landslide, the builders should have
   - **A.** built a huge overhang to protect the houses from the rain
   - **B.** planted grass everywhere on the hill to hold the soil in place
   - **C.** built the houses at the bottom of the hill after removing the plants
   - **D.** made the walls of the houses extra thick so the mud could not get in

3ME1.2 *assess the impact of safety devices that minimize the effects of forces in various human activities*

Safety Devices

There are forces all around you. A **force** is a push or pull that causes something to move. They act on you all the time. Every time you ride in a car, ride your bike, or walk down the street, forces are acting on you. If you trip and fall, the force of gravity pulls you toward the ground. If you are riding in a car and the car suddenly stops, your body keeps moving forward. These forces are powerful. Sometimes, you can be injured by these forces acting on your body.

People have created safety devices to protect themselves from these forces. A helmet protects your head in a fall on the ice. A seatbelt holds you in your seat. If you were in a car accident, the seatbelt may save your life. A basketball player wears special shoes. They have padding in the bottom of the shoe. These shoes protect their feet and legs from the force of pounding as they run on the floor. Many of these safety devices have stopped people from getting hurt. Others have saved people's lives.

You need to make sure you are wearing equipment that is meant for your sport. For example, a hockey helmet should be worn when you are skating. It is not designed to protect your head if you fall off your bicycle.

Safety equipment needs to fit you properly. This means that you need new safety equipment as you grow. Some equipment also needs to be replaced when it is old. All safety equipment must be replaced if it gets cracked in an accident. This equipment can not stop the forces that can hurt you the next time an accident happens. Choosing not to wear safety equipment can be dangerous.

A bicycle helmet is an important piece of safety equipment.

Use the following information to answer the next question

Ashley wants to ride her bike. She cannot find her bike helmet. She borrows her older brother's helmet instead. It is much bigger than hers.

3. What is the best reason that Ashley should **not** wear this helmet?
   - A. It does not fit her properly.
   - B. It is not the same colour as her own.
   - C. Her brother might get very angry that she borrowed it.
   - D. She might lose this helmet and have to buy two more instead of one.

Use the following information to answer the next question

4. This piece of protective equipment is meant to protect your

A. head if you fall off a bike

B. head if you fall on the ice

C. ears from very loud noises

D. eyes from harmful light rays

3ME3.1 *identify a force as a push or a pull that causes an object to move*

3ME3.2 *identify different kinds of forces*

IDENTIFYING FORCES

A *force* is a push or a pull that causes something to move. When you roll a ball across the floor, you are making the ball move. A **push** is when something moves away from the force that is making it move. A **pull** is when something moves toward the force that is making it move. When you pull a door open, the door moves toward you. Your hand is the force making the door move.

There are many different kinds of forces.

Gravity is a force that pulls everything toward the ground. When you fall, it is gravity that pulls you toward the floor.

Gravity pulls the ball toward the ground.

Electrostatic force is *static electricity*. Have you ever rubbed your sock feet on a carpet and then given someone a shock? That is static electricity. Static electricity is a force that can pull. You know this if you have ever taken off your tuque in the winter time and had your hair stand on end. Your hair was pulled toward your tuque.

Static electricity pulls your hair toward your tuque.

Magnetic force is the force of magnets. Magnetic force can push or pull. Magnets have two poles: a north pole and a south pole. If two north poles or two south poles are close together, they will push away from one another. If a north pole and a south pole are close together, they will pull toward one another.

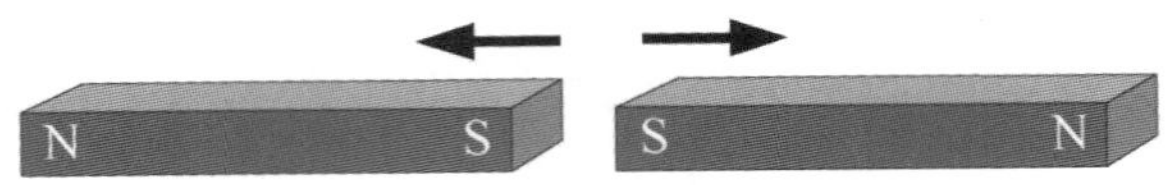

Two like poles push away from one another.

Metals such as iron, nickel, and cobalt are attracted to magnets. The magnets can pull these metals toward them.

Use the following information to answer the next question

These sled dogs are using a force to make the sled move forward.

5. The sled moves forward because of a
   - A. pulling force
   - B. turning force
   - C. twisting force
   - D. pushing force

Use the following information to answer the next question

This athlete is throwing a discus in a track and field meet. When she throws the discus, it travels 35 metres through the air before falling to the ground.

6. What force causes the discus to fall to the ground?
   - A. Electrostatic
   - B. Magnetic
   - C. Friction
   - D. Gravity

3ME3.3 *describe how different forces applied to an object at rest can cause the object to start, stop, attract, repel, or change direction*

3ME3.4 *explain how forces are exerted through direct contact or through interaction at a distance*

3ME2.2 *investigate forces that cause an object to start moving, stop moving, or change direction*

How Forces Work

There are forces acting on everything around you all the time. Even when an object is at rest, forces are acting on it.

An apple sitting on the table is at rest. It does not move because the force of gravity is greater than the other forces that might make it move. The force of gravity pulls it down to the table. The force of friction keeps it from sliding around on the table. These forces added together keep the apple still.

If you push the apple, you are adding a new force. The push force of your hand is greater than the force of friction. The forces are no longer balanced. The apple is now moving across the table. When you stop pushing, the apple stops moving. The forces are balanced again.

Your hand can change the direction of the apple while it is moving. By putting more force on one side of the apple, you can make the apple move in the other direction. If you put force on the right side of the apple, it will move to the left.

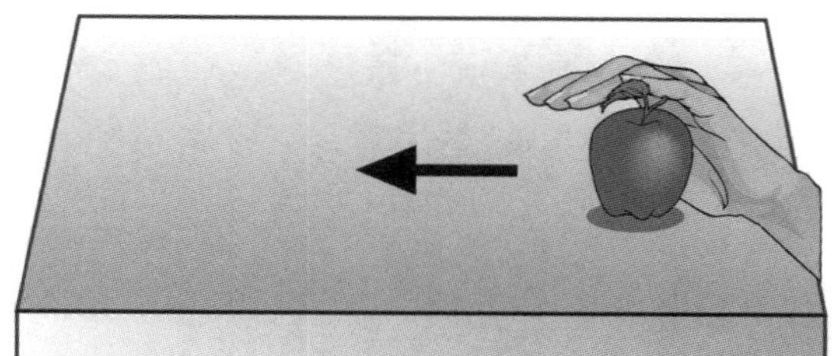

An object at rest will stay at rest unless an outside force starts it moving. A moving object will keep moving until an outside force makes it stop moving.

Some forces need to touch an object to make it stop, start moving, or change direction. In the example above, your hand gave the push force to start the apple moving. You used your muscles to push the apple. When your hand stopped pushing the apple, the apple stopped moving. Your hand has to touch a cup to make it move toward you. Your foot has to touch a soccer ball to send it in a different direction.

Friction is the force at work when two objects rub together. This force works when objects touch. Friction makes objects slow down. When a ball rolls down the sidewalk, it does not keep rolling forever. After a while, it comes to a stop. The friction of the ball moving against the sidewalk slows the ball down. Friction can make an object stop moving.

Other forces can act across a **distance**. A magnet does not need to touch another magnet to make it move. A magnetic field surrounds a magnet. Place a magnet near another magnet. You can feel the pull or push of the magnetic field.

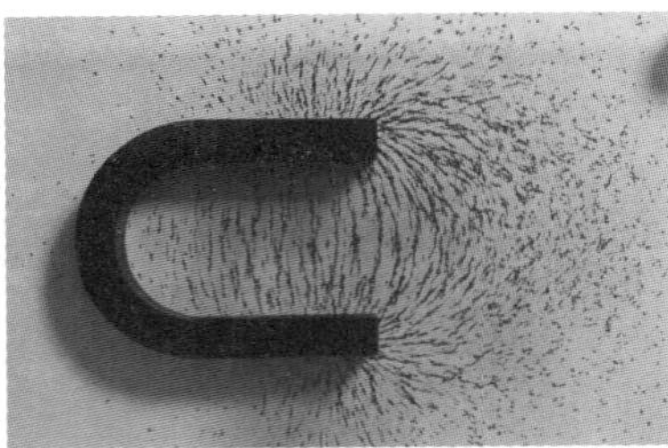

Another force that acts across a distance is gravity. A ball thrown in the air is still pulled back toward the ground while it is in the air. It does not have to be touching the ground for gravity to act on it.

Use the following information to answer the next question

Max was playing golf. He decided to practice his putting.

7. If Max hits the right side of the ball, it will **most likely**

   A. stop

   B. roll to the left

   C. spin in a circle

   D. move to the right

Use the following information to answer the next question

Neem's key is made of a metal that is attracted to magnets.

8. When he holds his key close to a magnet, Neem will **most likely** feel the key
   A. vibrating in his hand
   B. pulling toward the magnet
   C. moving away from the magnet
   D. spinning in a clockwise direction

Use the following information to answer the next question

Jane puts paper notes on the refrigerator door. She uses a magnet to hold the papers on.

9. The magnet sticks to the refrigerator door because the door is made of
   A. glass
   B. wood
   C. steel metal
   D. heavy plastic

Use the following information to answer the next question

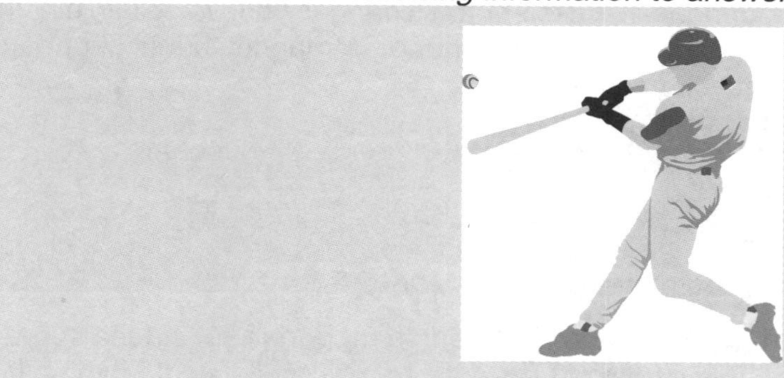

10. The force that caused the ball to start moving to the field came from
    A. air pushing the ball
    B. gravity pulling the ball forward
    C. friction from the ball and the bat
    D. the push of the bat hitting the ball

3ME3.5 *identify ways in which forces are used in their daily lives*

Forces in Your Daily Life

Forces act on you, and you use forces every day. You pull a door open. You push a drawer closed. Gravity holds you to Earth so you do not float away.

Magnetic force is used in things all around you. Electric can openers use a magnet to hold the can in place while it opens. Your refrigerator door is held tightly closed by magnets around the outside of the door. It is important that the cold air does not escape the refrigerator.

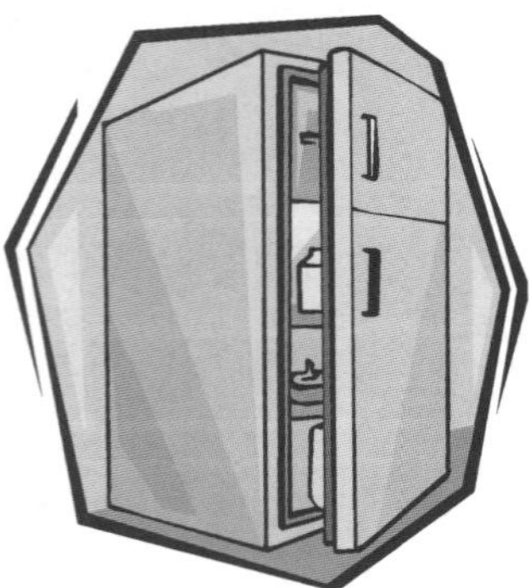

Magnets are used in the refrigerator door to make a tight seal.

Your telephone uses magnets. The microphone in the telephone changes your voice into electrical energy. The electricity travels through wires to another telephone. A magnet in this phone turns the electrical energy back into sound that you can hear.

Life on Earth would be very different without gravity. Gravity keeps everything pulled toward the ground. Imagine how tricky it would be to go through your day with no gravity. Sleeping would be difficult. You might float around and bump into things. On the International Space Station, there is little gravity. The beds are attached to the wall, and the astronauts zip themselves in.

With no gravity, it would be much harder to play catch with a ball. The ball might keep floating up and up.

A roller coaster uses only the power of gravity to keep it moving. A roller coaster does not use a motor to make the cars travel along the track. Gravity pulls the cars down the hills. The car builds up enough **speed** to carry it up the next hill or around a loop.

A roller coaster is powered only by gravity.

Friction is another force you use every day. The brakes on your bicycle use friction. The brakes squeeze the rim of the tire. This slows down the wheel and lets you stop.

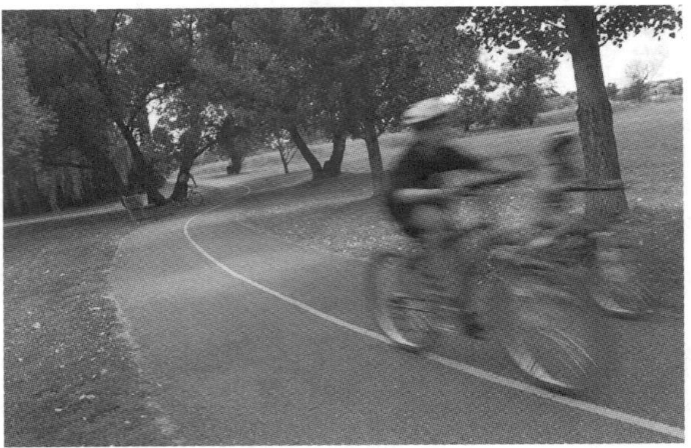

Friction keeps things from sliding around on you. Friction keeps the dishes on the table when you are setting it for dinner.

When you skate, you want to have less friction between your skates and the ice. If there were too much friction, you could not slide easily. As you skate, a thin layer of ice melts. You are able to move across the ice because this water lessens the friction.

Practice

Use the following information to answer the next question

Joan and Tony were cross-country skiing. Tony's skis slide along the snow easily, but Joan's skis keep sticking. Joan has to push harder to get her skis moving. She also finds that she is not able to ski as fast as Tony.

11. What is the **most likely** reason that Joan is not able to ski as fast as Tony?

A. There was more gravity between Joan's skis and the snow.

B. There was more friction between Joan's skis and the snow.

C. The snow under Tony's skis melted and increased the friction.

D. The snow under Joan's skis melted and increased the gravity.

Use the following information to answer the next question

Two groups of items are shown.

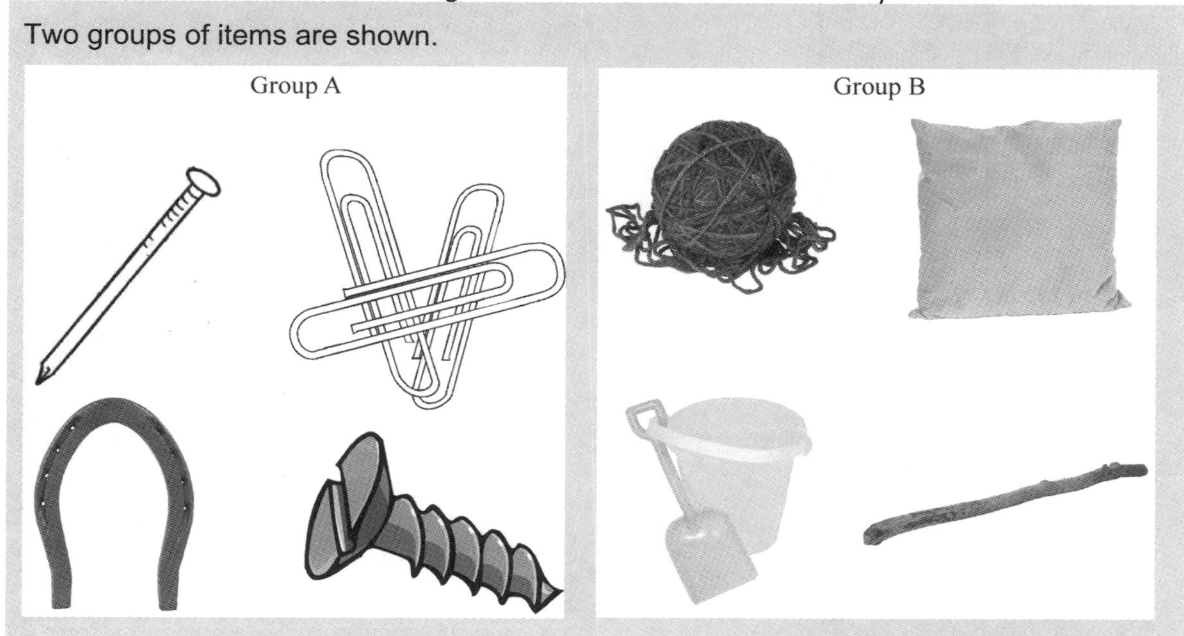

12. Which statement describes what the items in group A have in common?

A. They can not be picked up with a magnet.

B. None of them are attracted to magnets.

C. They are attracted to magnets.

D. None of them repel magnets.

3ME2.1 *follow established safety procedures during science and technology investigations*

Safety Rules

While you are learning about forces, you may be working with or building devices that use forces. Here are some safety rules. Your class may already be using some of them.

- Always be careful when bending, twisting, or stretching materials. Use eye protection when working with these materials. Something may snap or break. It could get in your eye.
- Watch out for your classmates. Never release a device toward a person. Some devices may have a lot of force. It could hurt someone.
- Be careful when working with heavy objects. Do not to drop them on anyone's foot.

13. When bending, twisting, or breaking materials, it is important to always

A. wear eye protection
B. use elastic materials
C. work with several partners
D. use as much force as possible

3ME2.3 *conduct investigations to determine the effects of increasing or decreasing the amount of force applied to an object*

Increasing and Decreasing Force

In science, doing **work** means to move something across a distance. Forces do work. A force moves something across a distance.

Increasing and decreasing force has an effect on the work. The more a force is increased, the more work it can do. When a force is decreased, it does less work.

Increasing a force may make something move faster. Pushing harder on a toy car will make it travel faster.

It may make it move more easily. Increasing force can make it easier to lift a heavy **load**.

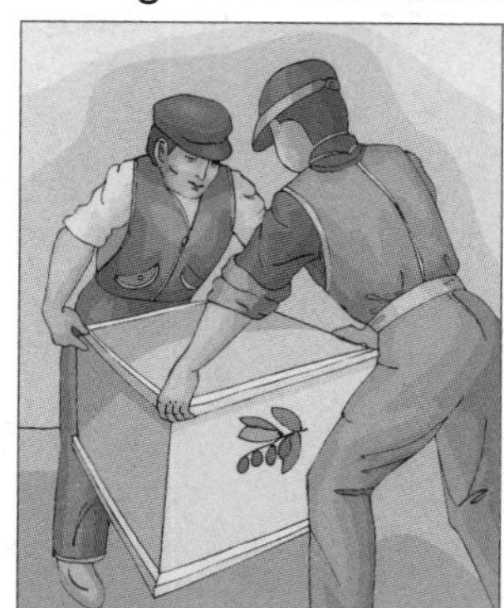

Try picking up paper clips with a magnet. How many did you get? See if using two magnets increases the force. You should be able to pick up more paper clips. Adding an extra magnet increases the magnetic force. A very strong magnet can lift a car!

Tug of war is a fun game. Each side tries to pull with more force to win. You might try to increase the force by pulling harder. You might try to increase the force by adding more people to your side.

There may be times when you need to decrease force. To stop your bike, you need to decrease the push force to slow down. You can decrease the force by pedalling more slowly. When you put on your brakes, you increase the friction force enough to stop your bike.

Practice

Use the following information to answer the next question

Marcia knows that by rubbing a balloon against a wool sweater 5 times, she can create a static charge.

14. Marcia could build up a bigger static charge by
    A. using a smaller balloon
    B. rubbing the balloon against the sweater 2 times
    C. rubbing the balloon against the sweater 10 times
    D. rubbing the balloon against a pair of denim jeans

Use the following information to answer the next question

Two teams decide to have a tug of war on the playground.

15. Team A will **most likely** win because they
    A. are pulling with more force than the other team
    B. have a better position on the playground
    C. all have better grips on the rope
    D. are holding more rope

3ME2.4 *use technological problem-solving skills, and knowledge acquired from previous investigations, to design and build devices that use forces to create controlled movement*

Designing and Building Devices That Use Forces

You can design and build your own device that uses forces to do work. Designing and building things can be a lot of fun. But before you start to build, you need to think about your device. Here are some questions you might ask yourself:

- What are you going to build? What will your device do? You may want to build a toy airplane that is powered by a rubber band. You may choose to build a boat that is controlled by magnets. You could build a crane or a marble run. All these devices use forces to do work. Remember, work is to move something across a distance.
- Does your whole device move, or does only a part of your device move? Your device may move or it may cause something to be moved. The entire model airplane moves through the air. But in a marble run, gravity pulls a marble through the track.
- What forces are being used in your device? Is it a pushing or pulling force? Will you use magnetic force? Electrostatic force? Gravity?
- How do the forces affect the movement?
- Before you start to build, take some time and write your ideas down. Decide what materials you will need and where you will get them. You may want to make a sketch or drawing of your device. Drawings can be a good way to think about and solve some problems before you begin.
- Will you need an adult's help?
- Test your device. Do not wait until you have completely finished building before you test. Each time you add a part or change something, test it again. If you wait until it is completely finished, it may be much harder to make small changes.
- How might your device be improved? Can you increase or decrease the force to make it work better? Will a change in the direction of the force make it work better?

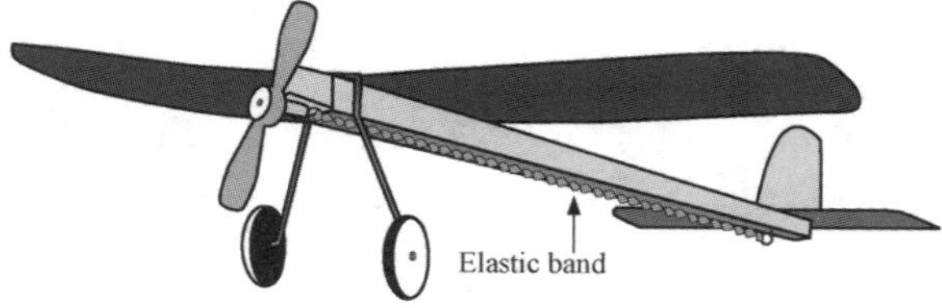

This airplane uses the force from a tightly wound elastic to fly. As the elastic unwinds, it turns the propeller. The propeller moves the airplane through the air. The more twists in the elastic, the more turns the propeller can make. If it is twisted too many times, the elastic can break.

Practice

Use the following information to answer the next question

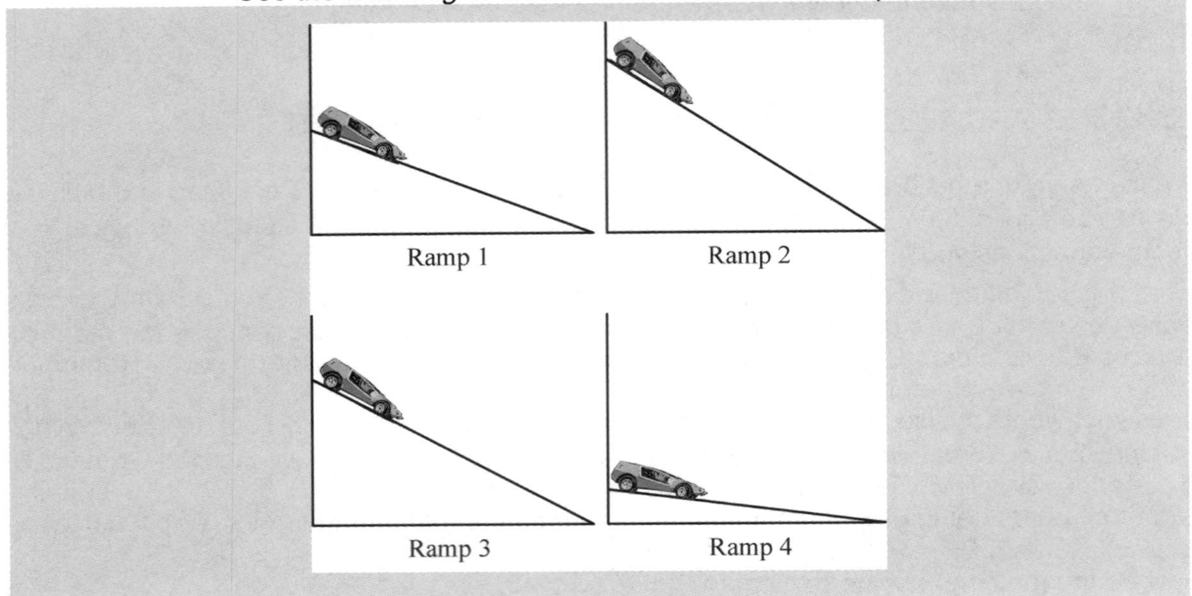

16. On which ramp will the car travel the **fastest**?

A. Ramp 1 **B.** Ramp 2 **C.** Ramp 3 **D.** Ramp 4

Use the following information to answer the next question

Rene built a model roller coaster out of a piece of tubing. He attached one end of the tubing to the wall. The other end was attached to the floor. He used a marble as a roller coaster car. When Rene dropped the marble, it did not stay on the track as it fell.

17. If Rene wants the marble to stay on the track, he should

A. start the roller coaster lower down on the wall and keep it just as steep

B. start the roller coaster higher up on the wall and keep it just as steep

C. make the roller coaster less steep

D. make the roller coaster steeper

3ME2.5 *use appropriate science and technology vocabulary, including push, pull, load, distance, and speed, in oral and written communication*

VOCABULARY

Please look in the glossary to find the following vocabulary words: **push**, **pull**, **load**, **distance**, and **speed**.

18. Sara threw a baseball a distance of 20 metres. Distance is

A. how fast an object is moving

B. how far an object has travelled

C. a force that pulls objects toward Earth

D. a force caused by a buildup of static electricity

Solutions–Matter and Energy: Forces Causing Movement

1. D	6. D	11. B	16. B
2. B	7. B	12. C	17. C
3. A	8. B	13. A	18. B
4. B	9. C	14. C	
5. A	10. D	15. A	

1. D

Soil can cause pollution in lakes and ponds. Water can wash away loose soil from an empty field. This can make it hard for plants and animals to live in the water.

2. B

When the new houses were built, all of the trees were removed. There was nothing to hold the soil in place. A sudden, heavy rainfall in the area caused a landslide. The builders should have planted fast-growing plants such as grass to hold the soil in place.

3. A

It is important to wear safety equipment that fits properly. Safety equipment was made to fit various sizes. Never wear any equipment that is too small or too big.

4. B

A hockey helmet is designed to protect your head if you fall on the ice. It is also designed to protect your head from getting hit with a puck or a stick. It should not be worn as protective equipment for anything but hockey.

5. A

A pulling force is a force that moves an object toward the force that is making it move. The dogs are using a pulling force to move the sled forward.

6. D

Gravity is the force that pulls objects toward Earth. The discus will travel for a distance through the air. Gravity will pull the discus toward the ground.

7. B

Hitting the golf ball on the right side will make the ball move to the left. Applying force to the golf ball on different sides makes the ball move in different directions.

8. B

There is a magnetic field that surrounds a magnet. Since Neem's key is attracted to magnets, the key will pull toward the magnet even when they are not touching.

9. C

Magnets stick to the refrigerator door because it is made of steel metal. Magnets can be used to post notes on steel, nickel, or cobalt metal objects.

10. D

The baseball player hit this ball with a bat. The push force of the bat sent the ball into the field.

11. B

Joan is not able to ski as fast as Tony because there is more friction between Joan's skis and the snow. Tony's skis slide along the snow easily. But the increased friction under Joan's skis made it harder for her to slide along the snow.

12. C

All of the objects in group A are attracted to magnets. A magnet will attract objects made of iron, nickel, and cobalt.

13. A

Use eye protection when working with materials. Something may snap or break. It could get in your eye.

14. C

She needs to rub the balloon against the wool sweater more times. If she rubs the balloon 10 times instead of 5, she would get a bigger charge.

15. A

Team A will most likely win because they have more people. Having more people on their team means they have more pulling force.

16. B

The car will travel the fastest on Ramp 2. This ramp is the steepest. Gravity will have a stronger pull on the model car. This makes it travel faster.

17. C

Rene needs to make the track less steep. The marble built up too much speed to stay on the track.

18. B

Distance refers to how far an object has travelled. In this case, the baseball travelled 20 metres.

Unit Test

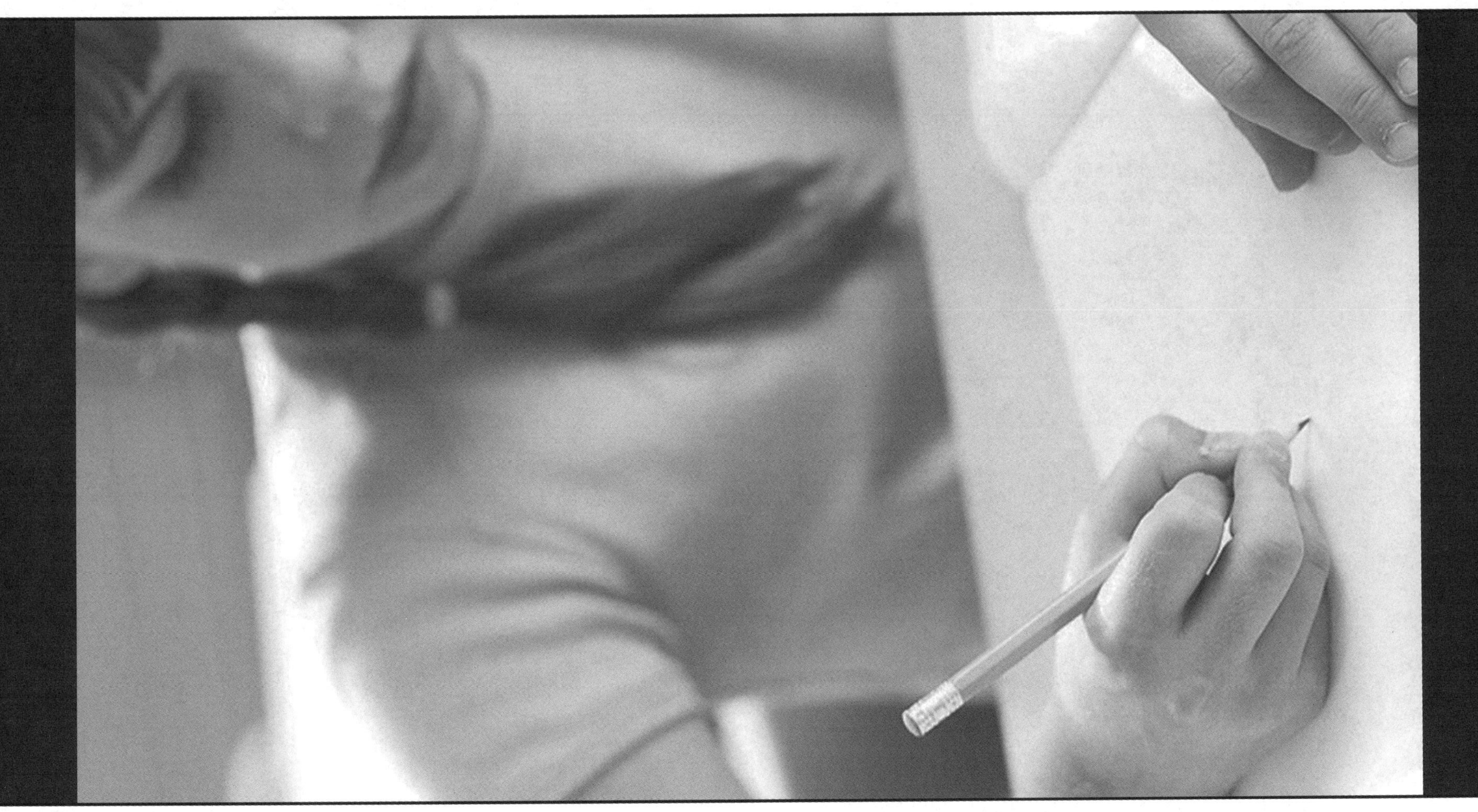

Use the following information to answer the next question

Ann used clay to make a dollhouse in her garden. The next day, it rained hard. Her dollhouse fell apart.

1. For what reason did the dollhouse fall apart?
   - A. Someone stepped on the house and broke it.
   - B. A strong wind blew the house over, and it broke.
   - C. The clay soaked up the rain water and fell apart.
   - D. The sun dried up the clay, and the house broke apart.

Use the following information to answer the next question

Daniel lives near a cattle farm. There are a lot of cows in the field. They have eaten most of the plants. After a heavy rain, Daniel noticed that a lot of the soil in the field had been washed away.

2. The soil washed away because the
   - A. soil of the farmland was not watered enough
   - B. short grass roots were not able to hold the soil in place
   - C. cows ate all the plants, leaving no roots to keep the soil in place
   - D. cows' hooves loosened the soil, making it easier to be washed or blown away

3. The piece of safety equipment designed to keep you safe in the car is called a
   - A. seatbelt
   - B. car alarm
   - C. windshield
   - D. seat protector

Use the following information to answer the next question

4. When this man pushes the cart of suitcases, the direction the cart moves is
   - A. toward the force that is used
   - B. away from the force that is used
   - C. to the left of the force that is used
   - D. to the right of the force that is used

Use the following information to answer the next question

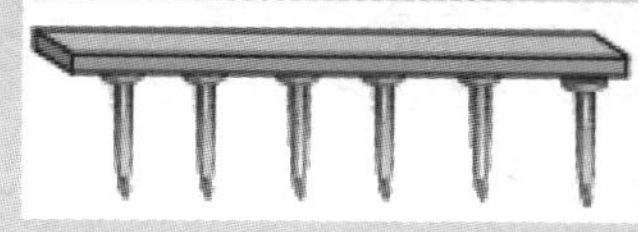

Veronica places a few nails on a magnet. She then turns the magnet upside down. The nails stay stuck to the magnet.

5. Which force keeps the nails attached to the magnet?
   A. Electrostatic
   B. Gravitational
   C. Frictional
   D. Magnetic

Use the following information to answer the next question

Kolbie pushed a wagon away from himself. It rolled down the sidewalk. It rolled for several metres and stopped.

6. What force stopped the wagon from rolling?
   A. Frictional force
   B. Muscular force
   C. Mechanical force
   D. Gravitational force

Use the following information to answer the next question

Eva brought a horseshoe magnet near a pile of paper clips. She noticed that the paper clips started moving toward the magnet before the two even touched.

7. What caused the paper clips to move toward the magnet before they touched?
   A. Gravity pulled the small paper clips toward the larger magnet.
   B. The magnetic field from the magnet pulled the paper clips.
   C. The magnetic field from the paper clips pulled the magnet.
   D. Air blew the paper clips upward.

Use the following information to answer the next question

Angus set his toy spring up at the top of a staircase in his house. He gave the spring a little push. It walked down the stairs of his house.

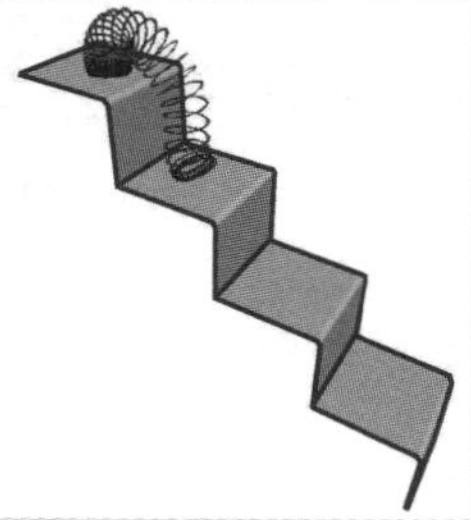

8. What force kept the toy moving down the stairs?
   A. Friction
   B. Gravity
   C. Thrust
   D. Wind

Use the following information to answer the next question

Two students are investigating forces. They drop a brick to the ground.

9. When carrying out this investigation, the students should take care **not** to

A. throw the brick too hard
B. drop the brick on their feet
C. let the brick get hot in the sun
D. let the brick get thrown into water

Use the following information to answer the next question

Sally built this toy car.

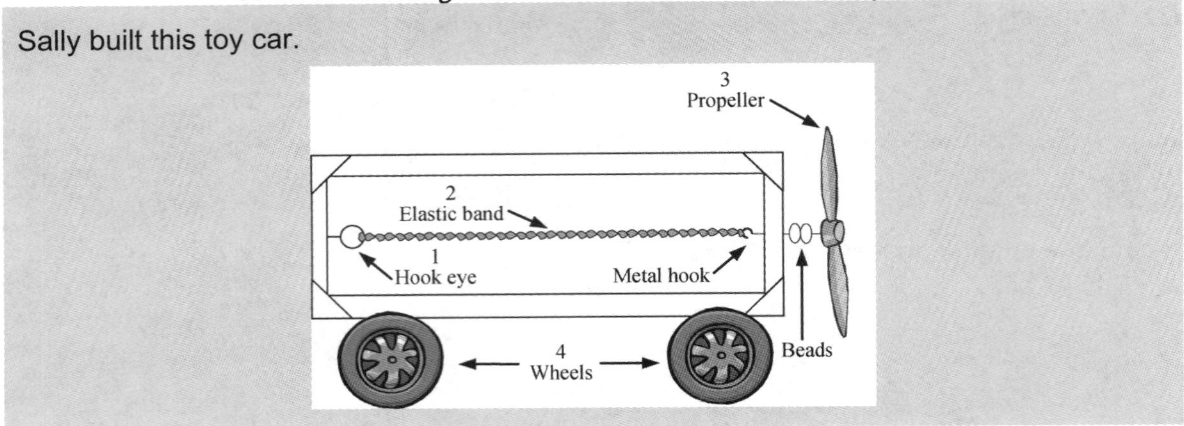

10. Which part gives the car the force needed to move forward?

A. 1
B. 2
C. 3
D. 4

Use the following information to answer the next question

Jill was playing soccer. The ball was rolling toward her. She put out her foot and stopped the ball from rolling.

11. The ball stopped rolling because the

A. pull force of Earth stopped the ball

B. force of gravity changed the direction of the ball

C. force of Jill's foot changed the motion of the ball

D. force of Jill's foot was in the same direction as the motion of the ball

Use the following information to answer the next question

Abdul spilled a bucket of nails. He is using a magnet to pick them up. This magnet can only hold a few at a time. Cleaning up the nails will take a long time.

12. To pick up more nails at a time, he should

A. cut his magnet in half

B. use a smaller magnet

C. use two magnets instead of one

D. use a different shaped magnet that is the same size

13. James needs to lift a heavy box. He knows that asking another person to help makes it easier because

A. there is more force to lift the box
B. they will have a better grip on it
C. there is less force to lift the box
D. the box gets smaller

Use the following information to answer the next question

Azlyn built a model car in science class. She wanted the model car to move. She placed it at the top of a ramp and let it go. The car sat for a moment and then moved down the ramp.

14. Azlyn's car moved down the ramp because

A. gravity pulled it down the ramp
B. friction pulled it down the ramp
C. a breeze pushed it down the ramp
D. magnetic force pulled it down the ramp

15. The forward movement of an object away from its resting spot is called

A. pull
B. push
C. gravity
D. friction

Solutions

1. C	5. D	9. B	13. A
2. C	6. A	10. B	14. A
3. A	7. B	11. C	15. B
4. B	8. B	12. C	

1. C

The clay house fell apart because it soaked up too much water. This caused the clay to weaken. It was not strong enough to keep the shape of the house, and it broke apart.

2. C

Since the cows ate all the plants, there were no roots to keep the soil in place. Too many cattle grazing in a field loosens the soil. This makes it easier to be washed or blown away.

3. A

Seatbelts are designed to keep you safe in a car. They may be uncomfortable to wear at times, but they can save your life.

4. B

A pushing force moves an object away from the force that is used to move the object. When this man pushes the cart, it will move away from the force that is used.

5. D

Nails are made of iron. Iron is a magnetic material. Magnetic materials are attracted to magnets. This attraction is called magnetic force. The nails are attached to the magnet because of magnetic force.

6. A

Friction stopped the wagon from rolling. Friction is the force when two objects rub against one another. It can cause objects to slow down.

7. B

The magnetic field from the magnet caused the paper clip to move. Some forces can act across a distance. The objects do not need to be touching one another. Certain metals can move toward magnets before they even touch. This is because magnets have a magnetic field that exists around the magnet. If those metals are in the magnetic field, they can be attracted to the magnet.

8. B

Gravity kept the toy spring moving. Gravity is the force that pulls objects toward Earth.

9. B

The students should take care not to drop the brick on their feet.

10. B

The elastic gives the force to move the car. As the elastic unwinds, it turns the propeller. The spinning propeller moves the car forward.

11. C

Jill's foot put a force on the ball. This force changed the forward motion of the ball. The ball stopped moving.

12. C

Using two magnets increases the amount of magnetic force on the nails. Abdul would be able to pick up more nails by using two magnets.

13. A

There is more force to lift the box with two people than with just one. This makes it easier to move things like heavy boxes.

14. A

The car moved down the ramp because of the force of gravity. Gravity is the force that pulls objects toward Earth.

15. B

Push is the forward movement of an object away from its resting spot.

NOTES

Soils in the Environment

Earth and Space Systems: Soils in the Environment

Table of Correlations

	Specific Expectation	Practice Questions	Unit Test Questions
3ESS1:STSE	Assess the impact of soils on society and the environment, and of society and the environment on soils;		
3ESS1.1	*assess the impact of soils on society and the environment, and suggest ways in which humans can enhance positive effects and/or lessen or prevent harmful effects*	1	1
3ESS1.2	*assess the impact of human action on soils, and suggest ways in which humans can affect soils positively and/or lessen or prevent harmful effects on soils*	2, 3	2
3ESS3:Concepts	Demonstrate an understanding of the composition of soils, the types of soils, and the relationship between soils and other living things.		
3ESS3.1	*identify and describe the different types of soils*	4, 5	3, 4
3ESS3.2	*identify additives that might be in soil but that cannot always be seen*	6	5
3ESS3.3	*describe the interdependence between the living and non-living things that make up soil*	9, 10	6
3ESS3.4	*describe ways in which the components of various soils enable the soil to provide shelter/ homes and/or nutrients for different kinds of living things*	11, 12	7
3ESS2:Skills	Investigate the composition and characteristics of different soils;		
3ESS2.1	*follow established safety procedures during science and technology investigations*	13	8
3ESS2.2	*investigate the components of soil, the condition of soil (e.g., wet, dry), and additives found in soil, using a variety of soil samples from different local environments, and explain how the different amounts of these components in a soil sample determine how the soil can be used*	7, 8	9, 10
3ESS2.3	*use scientific inquiry/experimentation skills, and knowledge and skills acquired from previous investigations, to determine which type(s) of soil will sustain life*	14, 15	11, 12
3ESS2.4	*investigate the process of composting, and explain some advantages and disadvantages of composting*	16, 17	13, 14
3ESS2.5	*use appropriate science and technology vocabulary, including clay, sand, loam, pebbles, earth materials, and soil, in oral and written communication*	18	15

3ESS1.1 *assess the impact of soils on society and the environment, and suggest ways in which humans can enhance positive effects and/or lessen or prevent harmful effects*

Soil Quality and Your Food

Plants are food for humans and animals. Soil is important to grow the plants. **Soil** is the loose material on the top layer of Earth. Plants get their water and mineral nutrients (chemicals) from the soil. The mineral nutrients in the soil are good for the plants. The plants are healthier and have more nutrition. Also, the plant's roots need soil to hold the plant in place.

Some soils do not have the mineral nutrients plants need. Sometimes, crops use up the mineral nutrients in the soil. Here are some ways that a farmer can add the missing mineral nutrients:

- Farmers could use **commercial fertilizers**. Fertilizers are chemicals that the farmer puts into the soil. The chemicals are the mineral nutrients that plants need.
- **Compost** is another type of fertilizer that farmers can use. Compost is made by letting plant matter rot. It is also called humus. Humus is an important part of the soil. Farmers can spread it on top of the soil. As water flows through it, the mineral nutrients seep into the soil.
- Farmers can rotate their crops. Each year, they grow a different crop or plant in another place. Different crops use different minerals. Some crops put mineral nutrients back in the soil. **Rotating crops** can keep the soil healthy.
- Farmers can let their field lie **fallow**. This means they do not plant anything in it for a while. Letting a field lie fallow lets the soil rest and rebuild itself.

A field lies fallow for a growing season.

Practice

Use the following information to answer the next question

Emily and Joseph bought two plants. Emily watered her plant every day and kept it in a sunny place. Joseph did the same with his plant. But Joseph also added a bit of fertilizer to the soil.

1. What would **most likely** happen to Joseph's plant compared to Emily's plant?
   A. Joseph's plant would grow faster than Emily's.
   B. Joseph's plant would grow slower than Emily's.
   C. Joseph's plant would die, and Emily's plant would stay alive.
   D. Joseph's plant would need less water and sunlight than Emily's plant.

3ESS1.2 *assess the impact of human action on soils, and suggest ways in which humans can affect soils positively and/or lessen or prevent harmful effects on soils*

Human Impact on Soils

The top layer of soil is the richest. It has the most mineral nutrients for growing plants. Good soil also has many spaces for air and water to move through it. People can damage the top layer of soil. When topsoil is disturbed, the structure of the soil changes. It cannot soak up water as easily. Air cannot get to the roots of plants.

As cities and towns grow, people need new buildings. These buildings are built by construction companies. Land is cleared of its trees and plants. Heavy machinery may drive over the soil and pack it together. Water and air can no longer get down into the soil. The roots of plants cannot get down into the soil. Water can flow easily over the surface and wash the soil away. The soil can pollute waterways like streams and rivers.

Many cities now have rules to protect soil. Construction companies try to disturb the topsoil as little as possible. They must try to cut down the amount of heavy machinery that drives over the soil. They must take steps to stop soil from washing away. But sometimes they must disturb the topsoil. When they are finished building, they fix the soil to make it like it was before.

Use the following information to answer the next question

Evan watched a construction site while returning from his school. Later that night, there was a big rain storm. The next day, Evan passed by the same construction site.

2. The soil at the construction site **most** likely
   - **A.** was full of plants
   - **B.** looked the same as before
   - **C.** had blown away in the storm
   - **D.** had washed away in the storm

Use the following information to answer the next question

There is a big field near Olivia's house. Many flowers grew there in spring. One summer, heavy machines drove through the field and packed the top soil down. The next spring, the flowers did not bloom in the field.

3. The flowers did not bloom because they
   - **A.** failed to get enough light
   - **B.** got more air than they needed
   - **C.** soaked up too much water and drowned
   - **D.** failed to get the nutrients they needed from the soil

3ESS3.1 *identify and describe the different types of soils*

Different Types of Soils

Most of the materials that make up soil used to be rocks. Over time, **weathering** breaks down rocks and minerals. It breaks them down into smaller and smaller pieces. Weathering is a very slow process. **Erosion** is the process that moves the rock pieces from one place to another. Wind and water can move the rock pieces. The rock pieces are smashed against other rocks and help break them down more.

Plants and animals also become part of the soil. When the plants and animals die, their bodies decay and mix with the rock pieces.

Sandy Soil

Look closely at a sample of **sand**. You can see the small pieces of rock. Sand is gritty. It does not hold together when you squish it in your hand. There is not much living matter in sandy soil. Sandy soil does not have many mineral nutrients. It drains well, but the water runs too quickly to be absorbed by plants. Not many plants grow well in sandy soil. Plants that do grow well have adaptations to help them survive.

Loamy Soil

Loamy soil is dark in colour. **Loam** has equal amounts of sand, silt, and clay. It is also rich in humus. Humus is the part of soil that used to be living. Humus is made from decayed plants and animals. It is rich in mineral nutrients. Loamy soil holds water well. It has room to let air get to the roots of plants. Many plants grow very well in loamy soil.

Clay Soil

The pieces in **clay** are much smaller than sand. They pack together tightly. Clay soils do not drain well. It is hard for plants to push their roots through. Clay is very sticky and holds together tightly. Clay is an **earth material** that is useful for building. It can be shaped and dried. People have used it to make dishes, musical instruments, and even build houses.

Use the following information to answer the next question

Mickey is a farmer and is very happy with the quality of soil in his field. The soil is very fertile and contains a good amount of water.

4. The soil present in Mickey's field is **most likely**

A. sand **B.** loam **C.** clay **D.** silt

5. Which of the following statements gives a reason why the weathering of rocks is important to support life on Earth?

A. Weathering helps to create rocks.

B. Weathering helps to produce soils.

C. Weathering helps to make mountains.

D. Weathering helps to create beaches for lakes.

3ESS3.2 *identify additives that might be in soil but that cannot always be seen*

3ESS2.2 *investigate the components of soil, the condition of soil (e.g., wet, dry), and additives found in soil, using a variety of soil samples from different local environments, and explain how the different amounts of these components in a soil sample determine how the soil can be used*

Identifying What is in Soil

Soil is made up of both living and non-living things.

The living part of soil is made up of small animals, bacteria, moulds, and decaying things. A dead leaf from a tree is no longer alive. But it is still grouped with living things in the soil because at one time it was alive. Rotting plants and animals are an important part of the soil.

Earthworms, small insects, and other tiny animals live in the soil. They eat plants and animals that have died. Animals that eat dead things are called **scavengers**. Scavengers break decaying plants and animals down into smaller parts.

Earthworms and other small creatures are an important part of the soil.

Bacteria and fungi are small organisms that also live in the soil. You cannot see bacteria without a microscope. Fungi are the moulds, mushrooms, and toadstools that you see growing on dead things. Bacteria and fungi break down the dead plants and animals into their smallest parts. Many of these parts are the mineral nutrients that the plant or animal used while it was growing. The bacteria break them down so the mineral nutrients can be used by new plants. Bacteria and fungi are called **decomposers**.

Non-living things are the parts of soil that were never alive. Most of the soil was once minerals and rocks. The pieces were broken off and worn down. Some are so small it is hard to see them without a magnifier. Some soil may have **pebbles** or larger rocks.

Soil also contains water and air. Water and air are not living things. They were never alive.

Healthy soil is made up of both living and non-living things.

Sometimes, people add things to soil. Pesticides and fertilizers are often found in soils used to grow food.

Pesticides are used to control insects and weeds. The insects may eat the plants. The weeds compete with the crops for space and mineral nutrients in the soil.

Fertilizers are added to the soil to help plants grow bigger. Fertilizers are mineral nutrients. Not all soils have the minerals that plants need. A farmer can add the missing mineral nutrients by using a fertilizer.

Salt is a common mineral. As water such as rivers flows over land, salt is dissolved in it. The rivers carry the salt in the water to the ocean. Ocean water is very salty. Sometimes the river water that carries the salt is used in farmers fields. Sometimes the rivers will overflow and flood the fields. When the water dries up, it leaves the salt behind in the soil. Over time, the salt can build up in the soil. Too much salt in the soil can kill plants.

Soil that is good for growing plants will have a healthy balance of living and non-living things.

Use the following information to answer the next question

Humans add chemicals such as fertilizers and pesticides to soil in fields. Nature can also adds chemicals to the soil.

6. What chemical found in nature is left behind from rivers flowing to the ocean?

A. Pebbles **B.** Loam **C.** Sand **D.** Salt

7. What gets recycled as nutrients for the soil?

A. Dead plants and animals
B. Plastic and metal litter
C. Sunlight
D. Rainfall

8. Bacteria are important to the soil because they
   A. eat the roots of plants
   B. take energy from plants
   C. make the mineral nutrients that plants use for energy
   D. break down dead material so the mineral nutrients can be used by new plants

3ESS3.3 *describe the interdependence between the living and non-living things that make up soil*

3ESS3.4 *describe ways in which the components of various soils enable the soil to provide shelter/ homes and/or nutrients for different kinds of living things*

How Living and Non-Living Things in Soil Are Important to Each Other

There are both living and non-living things in soil. The living things depend on the non-living parts to survive. Soil is a home and a source of food for many living things. These living things change the soil structure to allow water and air to move through more easily. Living things also put mineral nutrients back into the soil when they die. Both living and non-living things are important for the health of the soil.

Many small animals, such as insects and worms, live in soil. Some insects lay their eggs in soil. Larger animals, such as rabbits or moles, dig burrows in soil.

Some creatures eat the soil and the rotting plants and animals in the soil. Earthworms eat rotting plants. Their waste is called a cast. Earthworm casts help return some important mineral nutrients to the soil. The casts make up part of the humus in soil. Earthworms mix the soil as they move through. This is important for soil structure.

As small creatures move through the soil, they leave openings behind so water and air can move through the soil.

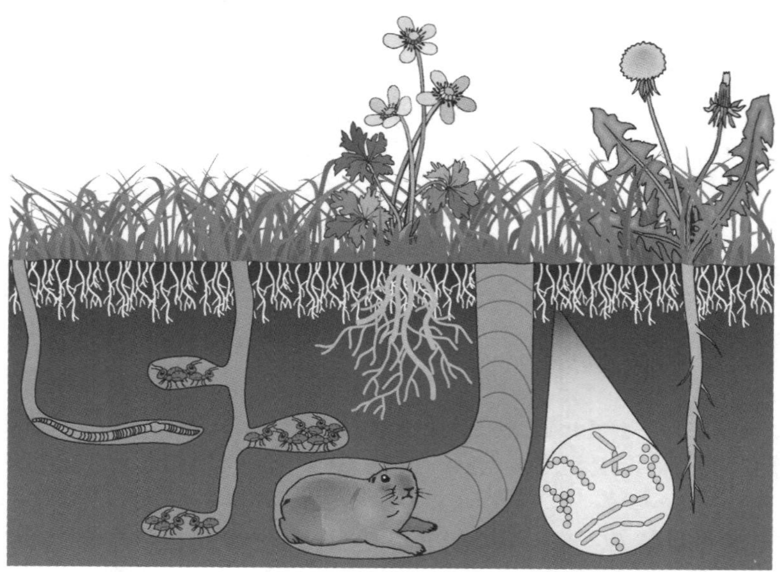

Bacteria and fungi are important residents of soil too. The mineral nutrients would not be returned to the soil without the decomposers. Decaying plants and animals form humus. The humus is important for soil structure. Soil that has humus does not pack together as tightly. Air and water can get through the soil more easily. It also makes it easier for plant roots to move through the soil.

Plants need soil to keep the plant standing. Some soil fungi work with the roots of plants to help them take in mineral nutrients from the soil. Plant roots hold the soil in place. Soil with no plants growing in it can be washed or blown away.

Practice

9. Soil with humus in it does not pack together tightly. This help the soil because

A. animals can dig farther into the soil

B. air and water can flow through more easily

C. carbon dioxide is able to flow to the surface of the soil

D. sunshine can travel farther down into the soil, helping organisms get energy

10. Which of the following statements describes a way in which earthworms are important to the soil?
   - **A.** Earthworms lay their eggs in the soil.
   - **B.** Earthworms help the soil hold more water.
   - **C.** Earthworms help the soil hold more nutrients.
   - **D.** Earthworms mix the soil as they move through it.

Use the following information to answer the next question

A farmer was frustrated with some insect pests. They kept eating her crops. She used a pesticide to get rid of the insects. The pesticide killed many of the other small animals living in the soil.

11. If there are no small animals in the soil, the **most likely** result is that the
   - **A.** soil will not pack together tightly
   - **B.** plants will grow much better
   - **C.** plants will not grow as well
   - **D.** soil will be healthier

12. Which of the following statements describes the reason why plants need soil?
   - **A.** The soil stops the roots from spreading.
   - **B.** Plants need soil to hold their roots in place.
   - **C.** Plants need soil to provide shade for their roots.
   - **D.** The soil prevents animals from eating the roots.

3ESS2.1 *follow established safety procedures during science and technology investigations*

Safety Rules

During this unit, you may do experiments on soils. Here are some safety rules to remember:

- If you are collecting soils from outside, always check the sample carefully before you work with it. There may be unsafe objects in the soil. If you find something, do not pick it up. Ask your teacher or another adult for help.
- It is a good idea to wear gloves while working with soils. But you should still wash your hands after handling them. There can be bacteria and other small organisms in the soil that can make you sick.

Use the following information to answer the next question

Deborah's family is building a new house. She would like to collect a soil sample to look at.

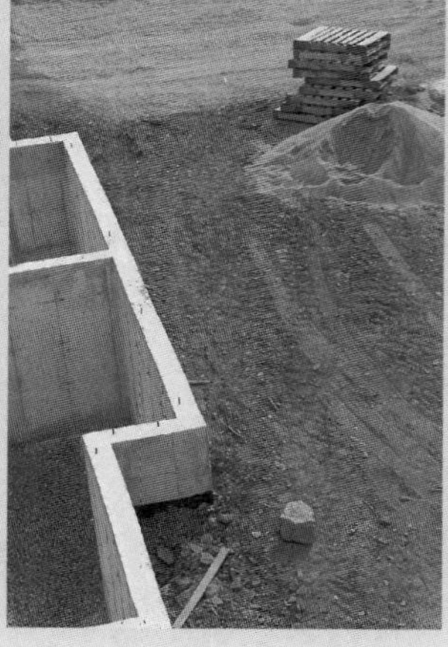

13. What is the first thing she should do before she starts to work with the soil?

A. Store it in the fridge.

B. Carefully check it for unsafe objects.

C. Add water to it so it is easier to look through.

D. Sift through the soil to look for any insects to collect.

3ESS2.3 *use scientific inquiry/experimentation skills, and knowledge and skills acquired from previous investigations, to determine which type(s) of soil will sustain life*

Investigating How Well Plants Grow in Different Soils

A science investigation always starts with a testable question. Your question might be "Do plants grow equally well in all soils?" You can design an experiment to test this idea.

Testing different soils

What do you think will happen in your experiment? You can make a prediction as to which soil you think will grow plants best. A prediction is a guess based on what you already know. Think about what you have already learned in school. Think about what you have noticed in the world around you.

Next, you should write down your plans for your experiment. You will need to decide the following things:

- What will you need to do the experiment? Make a list of materials. Remember, in a fair test, only one part of the test is changed each time. For example, in one test, you may decide to change just the type of soil. Make sure to use the same kind of seed. Give each plant the same amount of sun and water. Only the soil is changed. Everything else stays the same.
- What are the steps in your experiment? Write them down in order.
- Follow your plan. After planting, where will you keep the plants so they all get the same amount of sunshine? How much water will each plant get? How will you measure the plants? How will you record what you see?
- Record your observations. An observation is the information that you gather using your senses. You should record what you see, hear, and feel. Also, keep track of any measurements you need to make. Organize your observations. You may want to make a chart or graph of what you noticed.

These students have put the data from their experiment into a chart.

Once you are done your tests, look at your observations. Check your prediction. Were you correct? Write your conclusion. Your conclusion comes from the observations that you made in your experiment. A conclusion is the summary of what happened in your test. Which soil was the best for plant growth?

- If your results are different from what you expected, try to find out why. Give reasons why there was a difference.
- How would this information help others? For example, would this information help the custodian who is preparing the flower beds at school?

Practice

Use the following information to answer the next question

Ken decided to grow some radish plants at home. He predicted that radish seeds would grow better in garden soil than in sand. In each pot, he planted six radish seeds.

14. Which of the following diagrams shows what Ken should do to make this a fair test?

A.

Sand Garden soil

B.

Sand Garden soil

C.

Sand Garden soil

D.

Sand Garden soil

Use the following information to answer the next question

Ben was testing different soils to see how much water they could hold.

15. Which soil type will Ben find holds the **least** amount of water?

A. Silt B. Clay C. Sand D. Loam

3ESS2.4 *investigate the process of composting, and explain some advantages and disadvantages of composting*

Composting

Compost is the matter left over from plants that have died and rotted. Compost is very important in the soil. The mineral nutrients (chemicals) that were once in the plants are returned to the soil. Other plants can now use those mineral nutrients. This is good for your plants and good for the soil.

Overusing chemical fertilizers can damage soil over time. Compost is healthier for your soil. It adds mineral nutrients, but it also repairs the soil's structure. Composting food scraps and yard clippings means less waste is going to landfills.

However, there can be some problems with composting. Composting areas take up space. The more food scraps and yard waste your family makes, the more space you will need.

Compost can attract animals to your yard. Your composter should have sturdy sides and a lid. This will keep small pests, such as mice, out of your compost. Bury food scraps in the middle of the pile. This will keep away bigger pests, such as coyotes and bears. Indoor composters can attract fruit flies. Cover the food scraps with a layer of soil to stop the flies from laying their eggs.

Sometimes, compost can smell bad. This might mean that your compost is too wet. This can be fixed by mixing in some more dry matter, such as leaves or shredded used newspaper. It may not be getting enough air. You need to stir or turn your compost. If compost smells bad, something is wrong.

Collect food scraps from your kitchen in a small container.

The Contents of a Composter

Anything that was a part of a plant can go in your composter. You can compost food scraps such as fruit and vegetable peelings, coffee grounds, tea bags, and even eggshells. Yard waste, such as grass clippings and leaves, can also be composted. You should never put meat, oil, grease, or fat into your composter.

Over time, you will see the food scraps begin to break down. Eventually, the materials in your composter will become dark brown humus. Humus looks like soil. It has a rich, earthy smell.

You can mix your compost into the soil of houseplants or your garden. You can also put it on top of the soil around your plants. You can sprinkle it on your lawn. Humus can be used as potting soil.

Use the following information to answer the next question

Natalie was looking at everything her family throws away. She went through the compost pile and made a list of what she found.

Items in Compost

- Tea bags
- Pork chop
- Dead plant
- Leaves
- Potato peels

16. Which item on her list should **not** have been in the compost pile?

A. Tea bags **B.** Pork chop **C.** Dead plant **D.** Potato peels

Use the following information to answer the next question

Jackie knows that composting is good for the environment. She has a compost bin in her backyard. She puts her vegetable scraps and grass clippings in the bin.

17. The process of composting

A. removes poisons from materials

B. prevents the scraps from rotting

C. keeps the scraps from littering the environment

D. breaks down a material and adds nutrients to the soil

3ESS2.5 *use appropriate science and technology vocabulary, including clay, sand, loam, pebbles, earth materials, and soil, in oral and written communication*

VOCABULARY

Please look in the glossary to find the following vocabulary words: **clay**, **sand**, **loam**, **pebbles**, **earth materials**, and **soil**.

18. Which of the following statements **best** describes loam soil?

A. It is made up of minerals and tiny pieces of rock.

B. It is made up of equal parts of sand, silt, and clay.

C. It is very fine-grained and is sticky when wet but hard when dried.

D. It has had chemicals added to it to increase the size of farm crops.

SOLUTIONS–EARTH AND SPACE SYSTEMS: SOILS IN THE ENVIRONMENT

1. A	6. D	11. C	16. B
2. D	7. A	12. B	17. D
3. D	8. D	13. B	18. B
4. B	9. B	14. B	
5. B	10. D	15. C	

1. A

Joseph's plant would grow faster than Emily's. Fertilizers are chemicals that the farmer puts into the soil. They are the mineral nutrients plants need to grow.

2. D

The soil most likely washed away in the storm. Heavy machinery may drive over the soil and pack it together. Water and air can no longer get down into the soil. The roots of plants cannot get down into the soil. Water can flow easily over the surface and wash the soil away.

3. D

The flowers did not grow because they failed to get the nutrients the needed from the soil. Heavy machinery can drive over the soil and pack it together. Water and air can no longer get down into the soil. The roots of plants cannot get down into the soil.

4. B

Loam soil is the best for growing crops. It holds a good amount of water and has nutrients that plants need to grow.

5. B

Weathering is the breaking down of materials such as rocks and minerals. The broken-down rock debris made by weathering makes up most of the soil. Different kinds of rocks form different types of soil.

6. D

Salt is a common mineral (chemical) that dissolves in flowing water. More and more salt is added as rivers and streams travel to the ocean. Fields can get flooded with this water. When the water dries up the salt is left behind. Plants will not grow well or at all if there is too much salt in the soil.

7. A

Plant's bodies are made up of mineral nutrients. An animal's body is made up of mineral nutrients too. Animals eat plants or animals that eat plants. These mineral nutrients are returned to the soil when plants and animals die. Their bodies are broken down by decomposers, which return the nutrients to the soil.

8. D

Bacteria are important to the soil because they break down dead material. They break down the dead material into mineral nutrients. These nutrients can be used by new plants.

9. B

Humus allows air and water to get through the soil more easily. Humus is important for the soil structure.

10. D

As earthworms move through the soil, they help mix it. This is important for soil structure. It allows water and air to move through the soil more easily.

11. C

Plants may not grow as well if there are no small animals in the soil. Many of the small animals in the soil break down dead plants and animals into nutrients. These nutrients in the soil help plants grow. Many of these animals also help the soil's structure. This helps water and air get to the plant roots. The soil would not be as healthy if these animals were gone.

12. B

Plants and animals need soil. Plants need soil to hold their roots in place. Plants also help to hold soil in place. If there are no plants in soil, it can be washed or blown away more easily. Soil also has the mineral nutrients that plants need to grow.

13. B

Deborah should carefully check the soil for unsafe objects. Soil around a construction site may contain unsafe things such as nails or glass.

14. B

To keep a test fair, only change one part of a science experiment at a time. The only thing Ken should change is the type of dirt the seeds are planted in. Everything else should stay the same. Ken should give both pots the same amount of water and light. The size of the pot and where the plants are placed should also be the same.

15. C

Sandy soil holds the least amount of water. There is not much living matter in sand. It drains well, but the water runs too quickly to be absorbed by plants.

16. B

Meat should never be composted. Rotting meat will attract unwanted animals such as coyote and bears. Pork chops go in the garbage.

17. D

Composting happens in nature all the time. Dead material gets broken down into smaller parts. The mineral nutrients are returned to the soil.

18. B

Loamy soil is made up of equal parts of sand, silt, and clay. It sticks together better than sand but not as well as clay. Loamy soil holds water and nutrients well. It drains well. Air can reach the roots.

NOTES

Unit Test

1. The **main** reason farmers plant different crops on one plot of land each year is to
   A. keep the soil moist
   B. prevent soil pollution
   C. keep nutrients in the soil
   D. prevent soil erosion when it rains

Use the following information to answer the next question

A construction company builds a house in an area. The company wants to protect the soil in the rest of the area away from the house.

2. To protect the soil in the rest of the area, the construction company should
   A. drive heavy machinery over the topsoil to pack it down
   B. plant grass in the area to hold the soil in place
   C. spread the top soil out so it forms a thin layer
   D. flood the land so the extra soil washes away

3. Plants do not grow well in sandy soil because this type of soil
   A. is very sticky
   B. is very fertile
   C. cannot hold water
   D. has a lot of humus

4. Clay is used to make dishes and pots because it is a type of soil that is
   A. dry and loose
   B. extremely fertile
   C. sticks together well
   D. not able to hold water

Use the following information to answer the next question

Stewart's crops did not grow as big as last year. He thinks that the soil has less mineral nutrients than other years.

5. What should Stewart add to his soil this year to help grow larger crops?
   A. Pesticide
   B. Fertilizer
   C. Sand
   D. Salt

6. Which of the following charts correctly shows how plants and soil depend on one another?

A.

Plants	Soil
Give nutrients to the soil	Provides plants with sun energy

B.

Plants	Soil
Hold the soil in place	Holds the plant roots in place

C.

Plants	Soil
Eat bacteria that live in soil	Holds plant leaves in place

D.

Plants	Soil
Use soil to spread seeds	Plants feed bacteria that live in soil

7. Which of the following animals lives in soil?
   A. Bat
   B. Fish
   C. Tadpole
   D. Earthworm

8. The **most important** reason to wash your hands after you handle soil is that
   A. your clothes may get dirty
   B. the soil may stain your hands
   C. soil may be brought into your house
   D. there may be germs in the soil that could make you sick

9. Earthworms and small insects help soil by
   A. eating animals that take nutrients from soil
   B. taking in nutrients from the soil and giving it to plants
   C. breaking down dead plants and animals into smaller parts
   D. attaching to the roots of plants and giving them water and minerals

10. Soil that is good for growing plants will have
   A. only living things
   B. only non-living things
   C. a balance of living and non-living things
   D. a large amount of salt that has built up in the soil over time

Use the following information to answer the next question

Andrew wanted to try an experiment. Andrew took a plant out of its soil and put the roots in water. He made sure the plant got a lot of air and sun as well.

11. What else could Andrew do to make sure the plant stays alive?

A. Add nutrients to the water.

B. Replace the water every day.

C. Place the plant in a dark area.

D. Make sure to put the plant in a cold area at night.

Use the following information to answer the next question

Rachel wants to find out which type of soil will hold the most water. She plans to do an experiment.

12. The first thing Rachel needs to do when planning her experiment is to

A. ask a testable question

B. write down what she needs

C. record all of her observations

D. make a chart or a graph of what she notices

Use the following information to answer the next question

Bryan's family bought a new composter for his garden. They chose one with sturdy sides and a lid.

13. His family **most likely** chose this composter to

A. make sure the worms do not escape

B. keep small pests out of the compost

C. provide a good home for animals that feed on scraps

D. make sure that no one is able to climb inside the composter

14. Which of the following statements is a benefit of composting?

A. Less waste goes to landfills.

B. Composting takes up a lot of space.

C. More chemicals are put into the soil.

D. Compost can attract animals into the yard.

Use the following information to answer the next question

Parvana made this list.

- Sand
- Pebbles
- Gravel
- Small particles of rocks
- Silt
- Clay

15. What does the list describe?

A. Nutrients **B.** Compost **C.** Soil **D.** Lava

SOLUTIONS

1. C	5. B	9. C	13. B
2. B	6. B	10. C	14. A
3. C	7. D	11. A	15. C
4. C	8. D	12. A	

1. C
Planting different crops on one plot of land helps to keep the soil rich in mineral nutrients. Different plants take different mineral nutrients out of the soil. Some plants put certain nutrients back into the soil. By planting different crops each year, farmers can keep the soil healthy. Rotating crops can also prevent pests or bacteria from building up.

2. B
The construction company should plant grass seeds to hold the soil in place. The roots of the plants hold the soil so it will not wash away. This will also stop the wind from blowing the soil away.

3. C
Sandy soil is very dry and loose, so it cannot hold water. Since all plants need water to grow, they do not grow well in sandy soil.

4. C
Clay is very sticky. This characteristic makes it useful for making dishes and pots. The stickiness of the soil helps the pots to keep their shape.

5. B
Stewart should add fertilizer to the soil this year. Fertilizers are added to the soil to help plants grow bigger. Fertilizers are mineral nutrients.

6. B
Plant roots hold soil in place, and soil holds plant roots in place. Soil with no plants growing in it can be washed or blown away. Plants need the soil to hold their roots in place.

7. D
Earthworms live in soil. They provide nutrients for the soil and leave holes for air and water. This helps the soil.

8. D
It is important to wash your hands after handling soil because there can be bacteria or other small organisms in the soil that could make you sick.

9. C
Earthworms and small insects break down dead plants and animals into smaller parts. They are called scavengers. This makes the material easier to break down for the decomposers.

10. C
Soil that is good for growing plants will have a healthy balance of living and non-living things.

11. A
Andrew could add mineral nutrients to the water. Mineral nutrients help the plant stay healthy and grow strong. Plants usually get these nutrients from soil.

12. A
A science experiment always starts with a testable question. You can design an experiment to test this question.

13. B
Compost can attract small pests, such as mice. By having a composter with sturdy sides and a lid, you can keep these creatures out.

14. A
Composting food scraps and yard clippings means less waste is going to landfills.

15. C
The list describes soil. Soil is the loose material on the top layer of Earth. It is made of very small particles of rocks, pebbles, gravel, sand, silt, and clay.

Success on Tests

KEY STRATEGIES FOR SUCCESS ON TESTS

This section is all about the skills and strategies you need to be successful on tests. It is designed for you to use together with your classroom learning and assignments.

Finding Out About the Tests

Here are some questions you may wish to discuss with your teacher to help you prepare for quizzes and tests.

1. What will this test assess, or cover?
2. How much time do I have to write the test?
3. How important is this test to my final grade?
4. Are there any materials provided for the test?
5. What materials do I need to bring to write the test?
6. What kind of questions are on the test? Will they be multiple choice? Short answer?

Having a good understanding of effective test-taking skills can help you do well on tests. Being familiar with different types of questions may also help you.

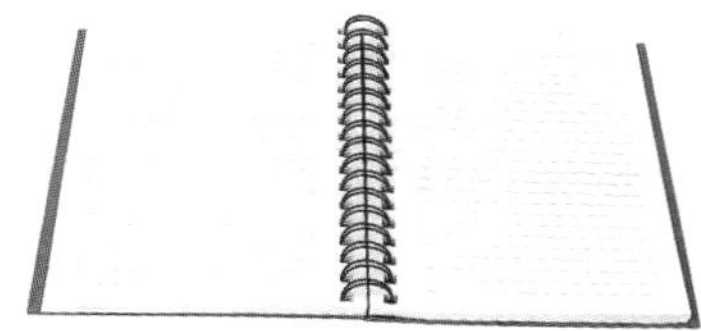

TEST PREPARATION AND TEST-TAKING SKILLS

Things to Consider When Taking a Test

- It is normal to feel anxious before you write a test. You can manage this anxiety by
    - thinking positive thoughts. Imagine yourself doing well on the test.
    - making a conscious effort to relax by taking several slow, deep, controlled breaths. Concentrate on the air going in and out of your body.
- Before you begin the test, ask questions if you are unsure of anything.
- Jot down key words or phrases from any instructions your teacher gives you.
- Look over the entire test to find out the number and kinds of questions on the test.
- Read each question closely and reread if necessary.
- Pay close attention to key vocabulary words. Sometimes these are **bolded** or *italicized*, and they are usually important words in the question.
- If you are putting your answers on an answer sheet, mark your answers carefully. Always print clearly. If you wish to change an answer, erase the mark completely and then ensure your final answer is darker than the one you have erased.
- Use highlighting to note directions, key words, and vocabulary that you find confusing or that are important to answering the question.
- Double-check to make sure you have answered everything before handing in your test.

When taking tests, students often overlook the easy words. Failure to pay close attention to these words can result in an incorrect answer. One way to avoid this is to be aware of these words and to underline, circle, or highlight them while you are taking the test.

Even though some words are easy to understand, they can change the meaning of the entire question, so it is important that you pay attention to them. Here are some examples.

All	**always**	**most likely**	**probably**	**best**	**not**
difference	**usually**	**except**	**most**	**unlikely**	**likely**

Example

1. All of the following animals are insects **except** for a

A. grasshopper

B. ladybug

C. spider

D. bee

Helpful Strategies for Answering Multiple-Choice Questions

A multiple-choice question gives you some information, and then asks you to select an answer from four choices. Each question has one correct answer. The other answers are distractors, which are incorrect. Below are some strategies to help you when answering multiple-choice questions.

- Quickly skim through the entire test. Find out how many questions there are and plan your time accordingly.
- Read and reread questions carefully. Underline key words and try to think of an answer before looking at the choices.
- If there is a graphic, look at the graphic, read the question, and go back to the graphic. Then, you may want to underline the important information from the question.
- Carefully read the choices. Read the question first and then each answer that goes with it.
- When choosing an answer, try to eliminate those choices that are clearly wrong or do not make sense.
- Some questions may ask you to select the best answer. These questions will always include words like **best**, **most appropriate**, or **most likely**. All of the answers will be correct to some degree, but one of the choices will be better than the others in some way. Carefully read all four choices before choosing the answer you think is the best.
- If you do not know the answer, or if the question does not make sense to you, it is better to guess than to leave it blank.
- Do not spend too much time on any one question. Make a mark (*) beside a difficult question and come back to it later. If you are leaving a question to come back to later, make sure you also leave the space on the answer sheet, if you are using one.
- Remember to go back to the difficult questions at the end of the test; sometimes clues are given throughout the test that will provide you with answers.
- Note any negative words like **no** or **not** and be sure your choice fits the question.
- Before changing an answer, *be sure* you have a very good reason to do so.
- Do not look for patterns on your answer sheet, if you are using one.

About Science Tests

What You Need to Know about Science Tests

To do well on a science test, you need to understand and apply your knowledge of scientific concepts. Reading skills can also make a difference in how well you perform. Reading skills can help you follow instructions and find key words, as well as read graphs, diagrams, and tables.

Science tests usually have two types of questions: knowledge questions and skill questions. Knowledge questions test for your understanding of science ideas. Skill questions test how you would use your science knowledge.

How You Can Prepare for Science Tests

Below are some strategies that are particular to preparing for and writing science tests.

- Note-taking is a good way to review and study important information from your class notes and textbook.
- Sketch a picture of the process or idea being described in a question. Drawing is helpful for learning and remembering concepts.

SUMMARY OF HOW TO BE SUCCESSFUL DURING A TEST

You may find some of the following strategies useful for writing a test.

- Take two or three deep breaths to help you relax.
- Read the directions carefully and underline, circle, or highlight any important words.
- Look over the entire test to understand what you will need to do.
- Budget your time.
- Begin with an easy question, or a question you know you can answer correctly, rather than following the numerical question order of the test.
- If you cannot remember how to answer a question, try repeating the deep breathing and physical relaxation activities first. Then, move on to visualization and positive self-talk to get yourself going.
- When answering a question with graphics (pictures, diagrams, tables, or graphs), look at the question carefully.
    - Read the title of the graphic and any key words.
    - Read the test question carefully to figure out what information you need to find in the graphic.
    - Go back to the graphic to find the information you need.
- Write down anything you remember about the subject on the reverse side of your test paper. This activity sometimes helps to remind you that you *do* know something and you *are* capable of writing the test.
- Look over your test when you have finished and double-check your answers to be sure you did not forget anything.

NOTES

Practice Tests

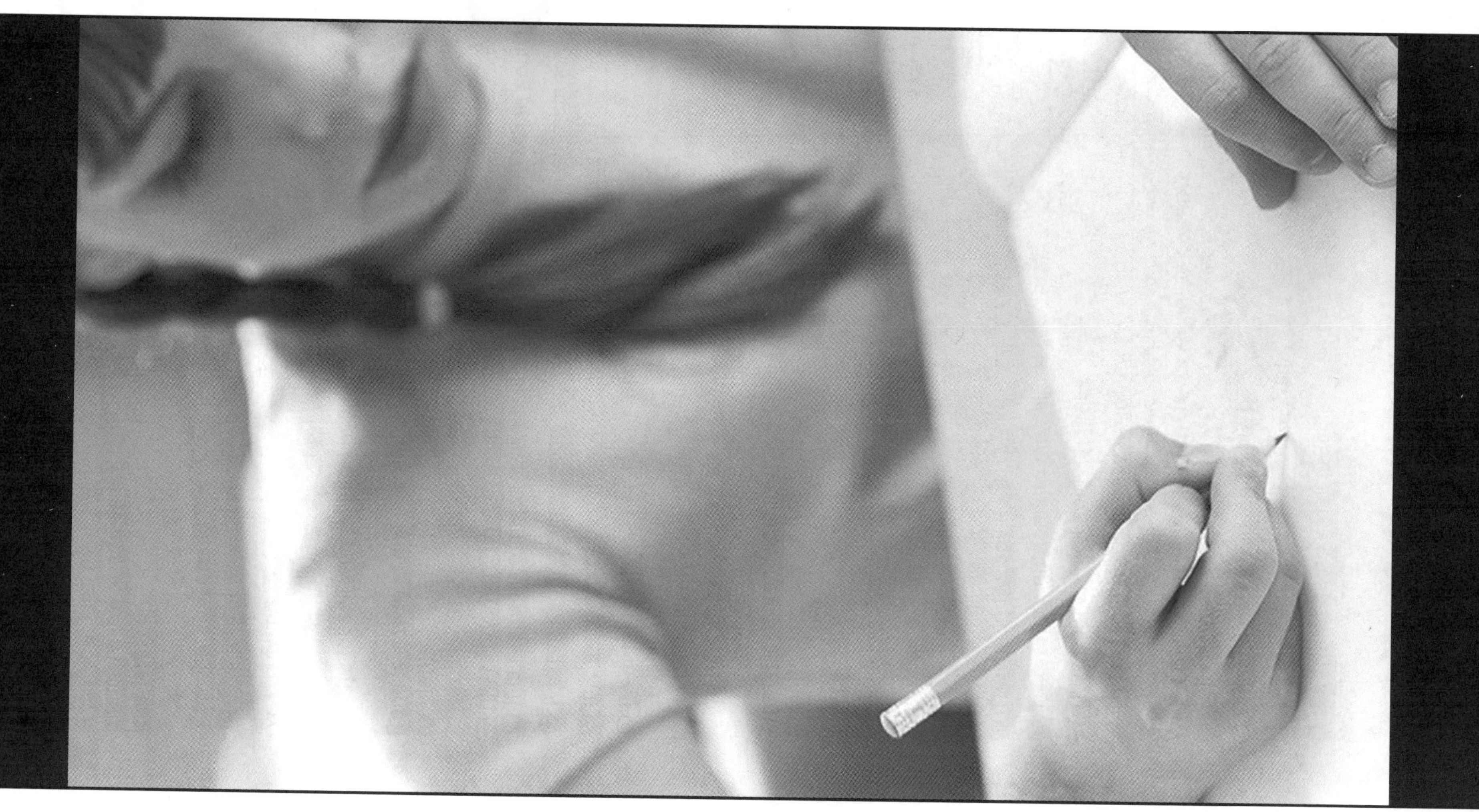

Practice Tests

Table of Correlations

	Specific Expectation	End of the Year Test
3LS1:STSE	Assess ways in which plants have an impact on society and the environment, and ways in which human activity has an impact on plant habitats;	
3LS1.1	*assess ways in which plants are important to humans and other living things, taking different points of view into consideration, and suggest ways in which humans can protect plants*	1
3LS1.2	*assess the impact of different human activities on plants, and list personal action they can take to minimize harmful effects and enhance good effects*	2
3SM1:STSE	Assess the importance of form, function, strenght, and stability in structures through time;	
3SM1.1	*assess effects of strong and stable structures on society and the environment*	11
3SM1.2	*assess the environmental impact of structures built by various animals and those built by humans*	12
3ME1:STSE	Assess the impact of various forces on society and the environment;	
3ME1.1	*assess the effects of the action of forces in nature on the natural and built environment, and identify ways in which human activities can reduce or enhance this impact*	21
3ME1.2	*assess the impact of safety devices that minimize the effects of forces in various human activities*	22
3ESS1:STSE	Assess the impact of soils on society and the environment, and of society and the environment on soils;	
3ESS1.1	*assess the impact of soils on society and the environment, and suggest ways in which humans can enhance positive effects and/or lessen or prevent harmful effects*	31
3ESS1.2	*assess the impact of human action on soils, and suggest ways in which humans can affect soils positively and/or lessen or prevent harmful effects on soils*	32
3LS3:Concepts	Demonstrate an understanding that plants grow and change and have distinct characteristics.	
3LS3.1	*describe the basic needs of plants, including air, water, light, warmth, and space*	3
3LS3.3	*describe the changes that different plants undergo in their life cycles*	4
3LS3.4	*describe how most plants get energy to live directly from the sun and how plants help other living things to get energy from the sun*	5
3LS3.6	*describe ways in which plants and animals depend on each other*	6
3LS3.7	*describe the different ways in which plants are grown for food, and explain the advantages and disadvantages of locally grown and organically produced food, including environmental benefits*	7
3LS3.8	*identify examples of environmental conditions that may threaten plant and animal survival*	8
3SM3:Concepts	Demonstrate an understanding of the concepts of structure, strength, and stability and the factors that affect them.	
3SM3.2	*identify structures in the natural environment and in the built environment*	13

	Specific Expectation	End of the Year Test
3SM3.5	*identify properties of materials that need to be considered when building structures*	14
3SM3.7	*describe ways to improve a structure's strength and stability*	15
3SM3.9	*describe ways in which different forces can affect the shape, balance, or position of structures*	16
3ME3:Concepts	Demonstrate an understanding of how forces cause movement and changes in movement.	
3ME3.2	*identify different kinds of forces*	23
3ME3.3	*describe how different forces applied to an object at rest can cause the object to start, stop, attract, repel, or change direction*	24
3ME3.4	*explain how forces are exerted through direct contact or through interaction at a distance*	25
3ME3.5	*identify ways in which forces are used in their daily lives*	26
3ESS3:Concepts	Demonstrate an understanding of the composition of soils, the types of soils, and the relationship between soils and other living things.	
3ESS3.1	*identify and describe the different types of soils*	33
3ESS3.2	*identify additives that might be in soil but that cannot always be seen*	34
3ESS3.3	*describe the interdependence between the living and non-living things that make up soil*	35
3ESS3.4	*describe ways in which the components of various soils enable the soil to provide shelter/ homes and/or nutrients for different kinds of living things*	36
3LS2:Skills	Investigate similarities and differences in the characteristics of various plants, and ways in which the characteristics of plants relate to the environment in which they grow;	
3LS2.2	*observe and compare the parts of a variety of plants*	9
3LS2.4	*investigate ways in which a variety of plants adapt and/or react to their environment, including changes in their environment, using a variety of methods*	10
3SM2:Skills	Investigate strong and stable structures to determine how their design and materials enable them to perform their load-bearing function;	
3SM2.2	*investigate, through experimentation, how various materials and construction techniques can be used to add strength to structures*	17
3SM2.3	*investigate, through experimentation, the effects of pushing, pulling, and other forces on the shape and stability of simple structures*	18
3SM2.4	*use technological problem-solving skills, and knowledge acquired from previous investigations, to design and build a strong and stable structure that serves a purpose*	19
3SM2.5	*use appropriate science and technology vocabulary, including compression, tension, strut, ties, strength, and stability, in oral and written communication*	20
3ME2:Skills	Investigate devices that use forces to create controlled movement;	
3ME2.2	*investigate forces that cause an object to start moving, stop moving, or change direction*	27
3ME2.3	*conduct investigations to determine the effects of increasing or decreasing the amount of force applied to an object*	28
3ME2.4	*use technological problem-solving skills, and knowledge acquired from previous investigations, to design and build devices that use forces to create controlled movement*	29

	Specific Expectation	End of the Year Test
3ME2.5	*use appropriate science and technology vocabulary, including push, pull, load, distance, and speed, in oral and written communication*	30
3ESS2:Skills	Investigate the composition and characteristics of different soils;	
3ESS2.2	*investigate the components of soil, the condition of soil (e.g., wet, dry), and additives found in soil, using a variety of soil samples from different local environments, and explain how the different amounts of these components in a soil sample determine how the soil can be used*	37
3ESS2.3	*use scientific inquiry/experimentation skills, and knowledge and skills acquired from previous investigations, to determine which type(s) of soil will sustain life*	38
3ESS2.4	*investigate the process of composting, and explain some advantages and disadvantages of composting*	39
3ESS2.5	*use appropriate science and technology vocabulary, including clay, sand, loam, pebbles, earth materials, and soil, in oral and written communication*	40

End of the Year Test

Ontario Science 3

End of the Year Test

1. Which of the following actions would **best** help a plant's habitat?

Ⓐ 

Picking flowers

Ⓑ 

Walking off trails

Ⓒ 

Planting new trees

Ⓓ 

Burning dead trees

2. Which statement **best** describes why walking or driving off trails and over plants is harmful?
   Ⓐ It can ruin tires.
   Ⓑ It takes a long time to clean shoes.
   Ⓒ It may accidentally kill an endangered plant.
   Ⓓ It causes the plants to use more water and soil.

3. Jared knows that the plants in his garden will start to grow in the spring. First, they need the snow to melt and the temperature to get warmer. On a cold winter day, Jared decides to put one of his indoor plants outside. He waters it and makes sure it is in a sunny location. The next day, Jared noticed that his indoor plant had died.

   What is the **most likely** reason that Jared's plant died?
   Ⓐ The plant got too much sunshine.
   Ⓑ The plant got too much air outside.
   Ⓒ It was too wet outside for the plant.
   Ⓓ It was too cold outside for the plant.

4.

This plant is in which part of its life cycle?

Ⓐ Seed

Ⓑ Adult

Ⓒ Flower

Ⓓ Sprout

5.

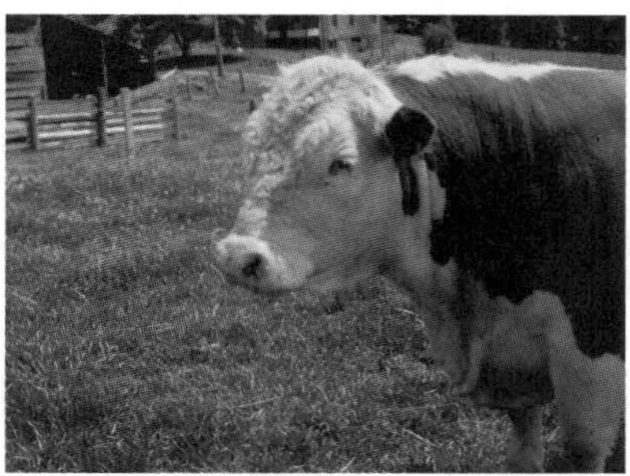

How do cows get their energy?

Ⓐ Cows hunt for prey.

Ⓑ They eat meat for energy.

Ⓒ Cows eat plants for energy.

Ⓓ They make their own food from sunlight.

6.

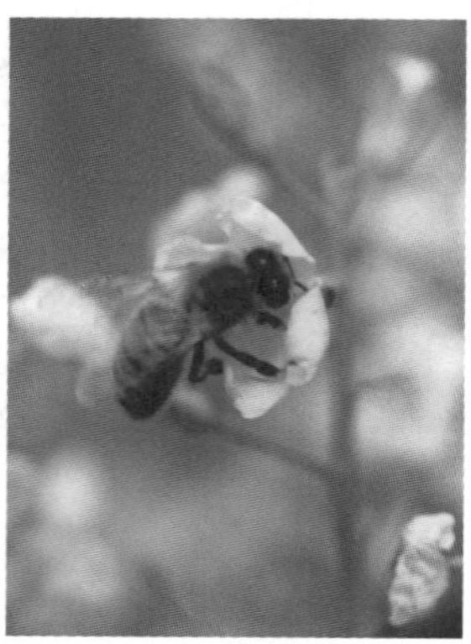

How does this insect help this flower to produce new seeds?

Ⓐ It provides the flower with food.

Ⓑ It provides the flower with oxygen.

Ⓒ It provides the flower with warmth needed to grow.

Ⓓ It provides the flower with pollen from other flowers.

7. Bill wants to grow some flowers in the early spring in Northern Ontario. Which of the following buildings would be **best** to grow the flowers in?

Ⓐ

Ⓑ

Ⓒ

Ⓓ

8.

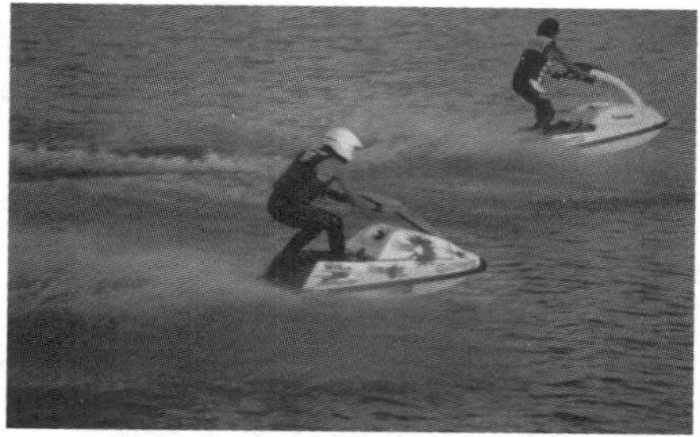

This type of watercraft is used near the shore in many lakes in Ontario.

Which of the following sentences explains the **most likely** way birds' nesting areas could be destroyed by watercraft?

Ⓐ The waves flood the nests, causing the eggs to be lost.

Ⓑ The noise of the engines shakes the nests apart.

Ⓒ The noise of the engines cracks all the eggs.

Ⓓ The waves drown any sleeping birds.

9.

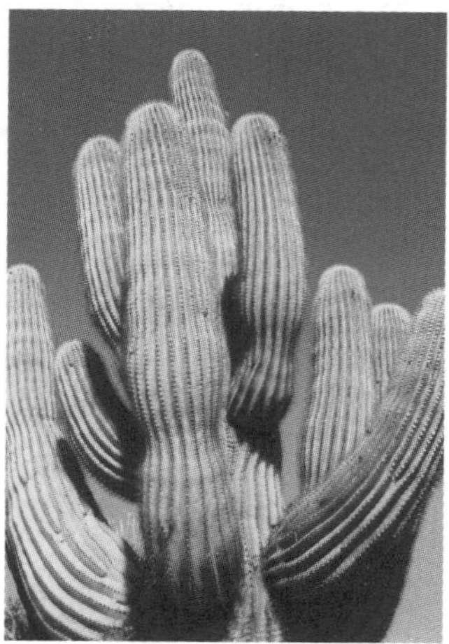

These plants have stems that are different than most other plants.

How is a cactus stem different from other plant stems?

Ⓐ They take in carbon dioxide.

Ⓑ Cactus stems produce flowers.

Ⓒ They store water for a long time.

Ⓓ Cactus stems have many leaves.

10. Which of the following seeds is **most likely** to be spread by animals?

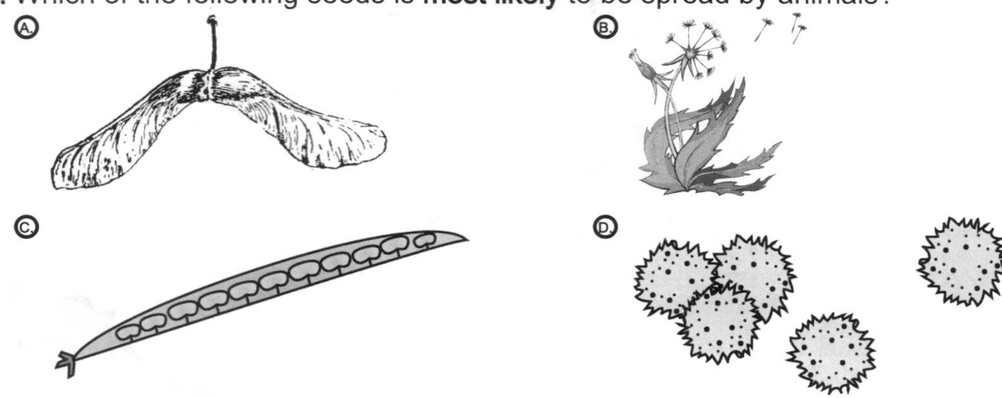

11. Jessie's father was buying shelves for the garage. He planned to store his heavy tools on the shelves.

What should Jessie's father think about **most** when he chooses the shelves?

Ⓐ The shelves must be strong enough to hold up the heavy tools.

Ⓑ The shelves must match the colour of the walls.

Ⓒ The shelves must be a lightweight material.

Ⓓ The shelves must be as tall as the ceiling.

12. People and animals often use the same natural materials to build structures.

Which natural material is used by both animals and people to build their homes?

Ⓐ Steel

Ⓑ Wood

Ⓒ Bricks

Ⓓ Cement

13. Which of the following structures is found in nature?

Ⓐ Shed

Ⓑ Igloo

Ⓒ Totem pole

Ⓓ Beaver dam

14.

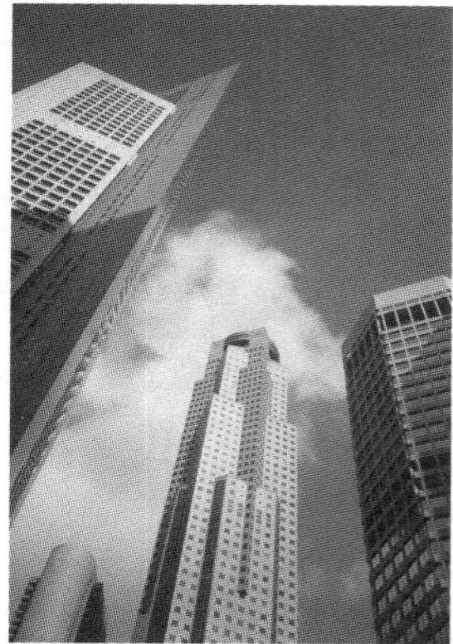

For what reason are skyscrapers built with flexible materials?

Ⓐ They must be able to bend in the wind.

Ⓑ They must be able to hold the weight of snow.

Ⓒ They must be able to have many different sized windows.

Ⓓ They must be able to hold more weight than they were designed to hold.

15. **Three Different Structures**

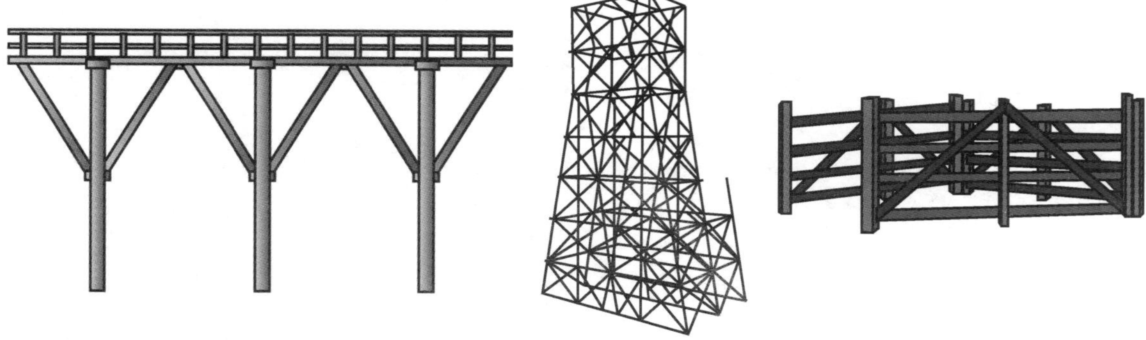

What is the same about these structures?

Ⓐ They are all towers.

Ⓑ They are all bridges.

Ⓒ The braces used in them make triangle shapes.

Ⓓ The braces used in them make rectangular shapes.

16. Lighthouses are towers that are used to help ships navigate in nearby waters. Lighthouses must be strong enough to stand up to the force of high winds near the ocean.

What is the **most likely** reason lighthouses are able to stand up to the force of high winds?

Ⓐ They are very tall.

Ⓑ They have a wide base.

Ⓒ They were made of brick.

Ⓓ They have wires supporting them.

17. Susan wants to improve the design of a bridge. She changes her design to use arches in her bridge.

What will happen to the bridge when Susan uses arches?

Ⓐ The bridge will be longer.

Ⓑ The bridge will be heavier.

Ⓒ The bridge will look better.

Ⓓ The bridge will be stronger.

18. James bought a large fish tank. He wanted to put the tank on top of a table. He knew the tank would be very heavy once he added the water.

What can James do to strengthen the table?

Ⓐ Push the table up against a wall.

Ⓑ Put a large bucket under the table.

Ⓒ Cover the table with a piece of metal.

Ⓓ Add pieces of wood to the legs to form triangles.

19. Jordan built a boot rack for his family so that they could store their boots when they were wet. The top shelf had to be strong enough to support the weight of the boots. Jordan did not want the boots to fall through.

Which of the following pictures shows the **best** design for the top shelf?

Ⓐ Ⓒ

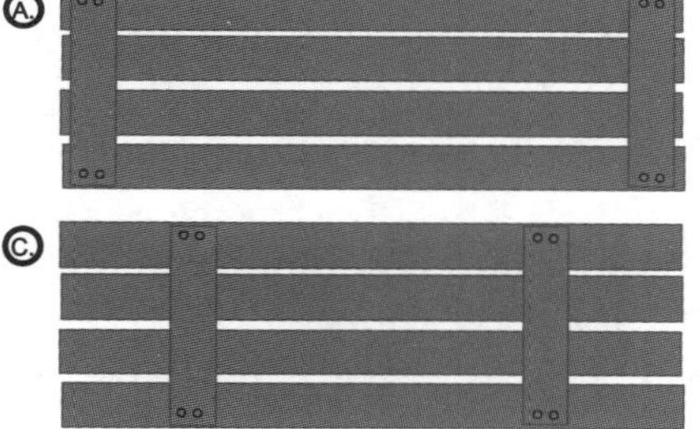

Ⓑ Ⓓ

20. What is the strength of a structure?

Ⓐ Its ability to carry a load

Ⓑ Its ability to stay balanced

Ⓒ Its ability to last a long time

Ⓓ Its ability to bend a little without breaking

Go On

Ontario Science 3

21. Heavy rain is washing away the soil in a field near Jacob's house. Jacob wants to stop the soil from washing away.

    Which of the following methods is the **best** way to stop soil erosion?
    Ⓐ Watering the field daily
    Ⓑ Planting more plants in the field
    Ⓒ Digging the field to loosen the soil
    Ⓓ Digging up the remaining plants in the field

22. What do basketball players wear to protect their feet and legs?
    Ⓐ Knee pads
    Ⓑ Long socks
    Ⓒ Shin guards
    Ⓓ Supportive shoes

23. Sasha was taking her clothes out of the dryer. One of her socks was stuck to her sweater. She pulled them apart. When Sasha pulled the sock from the sweater, she felt a small shock. She noticed that a force was pulling the sock toward the sweater.

    What force pulled the sock toward the sweater?
    Ⓐ Friction
    Ⓑ Gravity
    Ⓒ Magnetic
    Ⓓ Electrostatic

24. Andrea made a working model of a train. It has iron pieces in the front. A bar magnet is used to make the train travel forward.

    Which force moves the train forward?
    Ⓐ Electric
    Ⓑ Muscular
    Ⓒ Magnetic
    Ⓓ Gravitational

25. Kahlen was throwing stones into a lake. He noticed that the stones always fell into the water no matter how far he threw them.

For what reason did the stones always fall into the water?
Ⓐ They were too heavy.
Ⓑ Gravity pulled them toward Earth.
Ⓒ Friction with the water pulled them down.
Ⓓ The magnetic field of Earth pulled them down.

26.

Jennifer likes to go down the slide at the playground.

What force can slow her down as she slides down the slide?
Ⓐ Friction
Ⓑ Magnetism
Ⓒ Muscular force
Ⓓ Electrostatic force

27.

Sandra rolled a ball across a field. She needed to use force to make the ball move. This force had to be greater than the forces keeping the ball still.

How did Sandra get the ball moving?
Ⓐ Her push force was greater than gravity and friction.
Ⓑ Her push force was greater than gravity and magnetism.
Ⓒ The pull force she used was greater than electrostatic force and friction.
Ⓓ The pull force she used was greater than magnetic force and electrostatic force.

Go On

Ontario Science 3

28.

A hockey player is trying to get better at shooting the puck. Each time he takes a slap shot, he uses more force than the last time.

What difference will he notice each time he shoots the puck?

Ⓐ The puck moved faster than before.

Ⓑ The puck moved slower than before.

Ⓒ The puck changed direction several times.

Ⓓ The puck had the same speed each time he shot.

29. Tyler placed two same-sized magnets on top of two toy cars. He put them very close to one another.

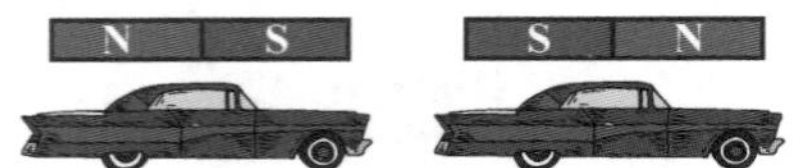

Which direction did the toy cars move?

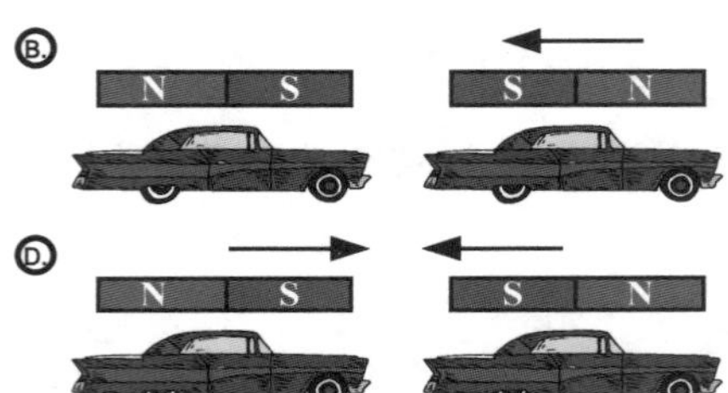

30. What is pull?

Ⓐ How fast an object moves

Ⓑ How far an object has travelled

Ⓒ The movement of an object toward a force

Ⓓ The movement of an object away from a force

31. For what reason do farmers use fertilizers on their crops?

Ⓐ To give the plants the nutrients they need

Ⓑ To help the plants stay upright in the soil

Ⓒ To stop the spread of diseases

Ⓓ To kill the weeds